Open Secret

MW01004206

To laugh, cry, and yearn for visions of things to come . . . to be inspired, to think, and to feel—all of these are a natural part of being human. To dream is a natural part of being human, too. This fluid aspect of our experience helps us to communicate on a deep level with our own spirits and with the magical universe that vibrates around us. It allows us to keep the doors to new possibilities open within ourselves.

Even though many of us sense the value of dreams intuitively, we often don't remember them or we find them strange, chaotic, and distant from our understanding.

This book can help. It will teach you how to remember your dreams more clearly, how to understand them, and how to see them in relationship to the rest of your life. It will not interpret dream images for you or give you some old, worn-out "dictionary definitions" with which to re-label your dream images. It will, however, empower you, encourage you to view dream exploration as an adventure, and provide you with the tools you need to absorb the messages in your dreams. Read this book and reclaim the vibrant, creative part of yourself that dreams!

An Invitation to Dream

Tap the Resources of Inner Wisdom

Ana Lora Garrard

1993
Llewellyn Publications
St. Paul, Minnesota 55164-0383, U.S.A.

FIRST EDITION
Second Printing, 1993

Cover art: Ana Lora Garrard
Illustrations: Ana Lora Garrard
Cover Design: Christopher Wells

Library of Congress Cataloging-in-Publication Data
    Garrard, Ana Lora.
        An invitation to dream: tap the resources of inner wisdom / by Ana Lora Garrard
        p.   cm.
        ISBN 0-87542-253-5
        1. Dreams. 2. Dream interpretation. I. Title.
    BF1091.G377   1993
    154.6'3--dc20   93-4924
                                                CIP

Printed on recycled paper with soy ink

Llewellyn Publications
A Division of Llewellyn Worldwide, Ltd.
P. O. Box 64383, St. Paul, MN 55164-0383

About the Author

Ana Lora Garrard is a teacher, artist, and writer. She was born in Syracuse, New York, on July 1, 1958, and gradually made her way across the country until she reached her present home in the forested, coastal lands of northern California.

Ana Lora has taught workshops on understanding dreams privately and in universities, hospices, and healing centers for ten years. She believes in the innate beauty and wisdom of the human spirit and she feels that a good teacher is one who helps us to recognize this beauty and wisdom in ourselves.

To Write to the Author

If you wish to contact the author or would like more information about this book, please write to the author in care of Llewellyn Worldwide, and we will forward your request. Both the author and publisher appreciate hearing from you and learning of your enjoyment of this book and how it has helped you. Llewellyn Worldwide cannot guarantee that every letter written to the author can be answered, but all will be forwarded. Please write to:

Ana Lora Garrard
c/o Llewellyn Worldwide
P.O. Box 64383-253, St. Paul, MN 55164-0383, U.S.A.

Please enclosed a self-addressed, stamped envelope or $1.00 to cover costs.
If outside the U.S.A., enclose international postal reply coupon.

Free Catalog from Llewellyn

For more than 90 years Llewellyn has brought its readers knowledge in the fields of metaphysics and human potential. Learn about the newest books in spiritual guidance, natural healing, astrology, occult philosophy and more. Enjoy book reviews, new age articles, a calendar of events, plus current advertised products and services. To get your free copy of *Llewellyn's New Worlds of Mind and Spirit*, send your name and address to:

Llewellyn's New Worlds of Mind and Spirit
P.O. Box 64383-253, St. Paul, MN 55164-0383, U.S.A.

The artwork in this book was inspired by the dreams of the author.

This book is dedicated to all my friends
in *this* world and others.

Table of Contents

Introduction

The Meaning of Dreams

For years I had trouble with questions such as, "What do dreams mean?" or "What does *this* dream mean?" Whenever I gave lectures on dreams I'd read my definition of them from a piece of paper because I couldn't remember what I wanted to say. The words I'd carefully written out were always elaborate ones that I'm fairly sure no one understood. Deep down inside, I knew that I didn't really understand what I was saying, either.

Even though I'd been teaching about dreams for a long time, I still couldn't define them or analyze them at someone's request. I knew how to guide people through the process of understanding their dreams, yet, repeatedly, I discovered that I didn't know how to talk *about* them at all. Dreams always reminded me of warm breezes and winter starlight and butterflies fluttering around my ears. Every time I tried to nail them down with labels or cute phrases, they danced away from me.

When I was younger, this frustrated me immensely because I felt that I had a responsibility as a dream class teacher to be able to pinpoint dreams in a precise and elegant way. Yet whenever I'd run into people who'd ask me to interpret their dreams or explain to them what dreams were all about, all I could do was blush and mumble something unintelligible.

One such incident I can clearly recall, happened after I had gone to a restaurant with a friend of mine. My friend and I were just sitting down with drinks when she saw a group of about eight people she knew. They beckoned to us to join them, so we went over and squeezed in around their table. Right away my friend introduced me by saying, "This is Ana Lora, my dream class teacher."

Just as I feared, one of the men who had been drinking quite a bit perked up, burped a little to himself, and smiled at me. Leaning toward me, he asked affably, "Hey, since you're the Dream Lady, tell me, what do dreams mean anyway?"

I looked down in embarrassment and wished that man could have popped and disappeared, like one of the bubbles in my drink, before he had a chance to ask that question. As I searched for words, I realized that half the table was waiting for my answer. All I could think of was my fluttering, elusive butterflies. Nowhere in my mental landscape could I find an answer to that question that looked like it might shape itself into ten easy words or less.

Finally, I smiled innocently at my questioner and asked, "What do *you* think they mean?" Immediately the man began telling me everything he'd ever read or thought about dreams. Then he went on and told me all the dreams that he, his brother, or his girlfriend had had for the last six years. I breathed a sigh of relief. I was off the hook.

It took me a long time to realize consciously what I had always known intuitively in those days — that I did not need to try to interpret others' dreams or make any absolute statements about their meaning in order to teach about them. Eventually it dawned on me, however, that saying "A dream means this and only this," is just like saying "Life means this and only this." No true artist, teacher, or lover ever says that kind of thing. I didn't need to say it, either.

Dream understanding is a journey, a path of discovery, not a set of formulas. Now that I truly recognize this, I can respond to someone who asks me to analyze a dream *for* them by suggesting that we sit down and explore that dream together, so that the person can begin to understand what the dream means to them personally. And when I teach workshops, I usually tell my students, "I don't know all the different creative dream journeys you could possibly take. In your dreams, you will hear symphonies that I will never hear exactly as you hear them, and you will see crystal clear blue lakes that I will never see in the way that you see them. I do, however, know some things about dreams that I think will help you in your own explorations of them."

In this same spirit, I now offer you, my reader, some basic information about how dreams work, ways of remembering them more clearly, descriptions of different adventures you could embark upon with them, and the story of my own personal dream journey. Beyond that, all I want to say is that I wish you happiness in your continuing discovery of the meaning of your own dreams. Remember to trust yourself.

1

Questions and Answers

Right now you stand on the threshold of a new dream journey. The nature of this journey is up to you. You may just read through these pages, discover a fresh perspective on your dreams, and then decide that your journey is complete . . . or you may start feeling so excited about understanding your dreams that you choose to go on and use the tools in this book to explore your dreams' messages.

Yet whatever shape your dream journey takes, this first chapter should be both helpful and inspiring. It contains my responses to the twelve questions I have been asked most often during dream lectures and workshops. Perhaps you will find answers to some of your own questions within it.

1. What are dreams?

Dreams are warm breezes and winter starlight and butterflies fluttering around our ears. They are the friends we haven't met yet and the wisdom living inside us we forgot we knew.

In other words, dreams are the new visions that come to us when we let go of limitations in what we will *allow* ourselves to experience. They are not just strange pictures that sprout randomly in our minds. They are not "separate" from ourselves. They are simply a larger way of seeing. Any time we release barriers to a full, direct, rich experience of ourselves and our world, we begin to dream.

Many of us participate in a form of dreaming while we are awake just by walking in a meadow, feeling the wind on our faces and the beating of our own hearts. Others enter waking dreams through meditation, flashes of creative inspiration, moments of listening to our intuition, trances, hypnosis sessions, drug experiments, visualizations, and daydreams. In all of these experiences, just as in "sleeping" dreams, we let go of our usual mental constraints and step through the doorway into a new, enhanced dimension of awareness.

The only difference between sleeping dreams and waking dreams is a matter of degree. Because we identify less closely with our bodies and the Self that we know while we sleep, we are apt to dream more deeply at that time. It's easier to release more barriers to our perceptions while we are asleep. Yet dreaming is still a gift that we can give ourselves at any moment.

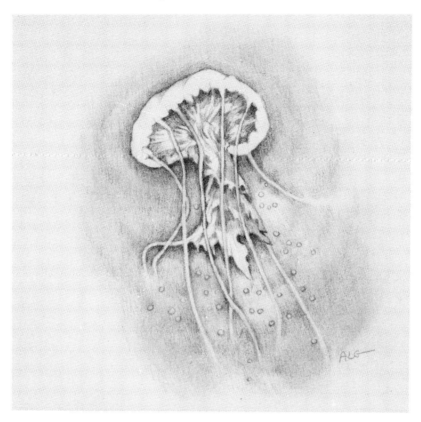

2. What happens when we dream?

To understand how our sleeping dreams work, we must first take a look at the role they play in our waking lives.

While we are awake, most of us build some protective walls around ourselves. "These are my limits," we say. "Everything else is beyond me."

Yet none of us live inside walls that are truly permanent. Life won't let us. In the long range those walls will crumble, whether by the force of new inspiration or by the apparent pressure of "outside circumstances." We will shed our old ideas when we have out-grown them, just as a snake sheds its skin.

On a short-term basis, however, a time comes at least once every 18 hours or so when we feel the need to lay these barriers down temporarily. We get tired of holding them up. We yearn for the release found in the dream state.

When we do give in to this yearning and drift off to sleep at night, we surrender the control we normally keep over our perceptions. This greater openness and receptivity allows us to see parts of ourselves we have denied or forgotten. Thus, as we begin to dream, we see images of ourselves or someone like us, longing to dance . . . expressing anger and frustration . . . or responding fully and compassionately to someone who needs our help. Our dreams show us both the humanness in us that feels the need to create barriers *and* the divinity in us that gently presses us to grow and release those barriers.

When the time comes for us to wake up, our attention narrows once again and we begin to refocus on the events within our physical experience. However, as we awaken, we can remain for some time in a transitional state in which our attention is delicately balanced between our dreams and our physical reality. If we don't force our attention back to an exclusive, physical focus then, we can stay in contact with our dreams and begin to record them. This allows us to start building a bridge between our expanded, nighttime visions and our daily, physical experience.

3. Why do we dream about certain images?

Every dream image we draw forth helps to reawaken something sleeping below the surface of our awareness with which we need to make contact. The color, shape, sound, texture, feel, and intensity of the image all help to make some forgotten part of ourselves more real.

Many of us have become numb to our own feelings and deaf to the voices of our own spirits. Dream images help to wake us up again. They help us to feel and hear and see more fully — as we were meant to feel and hear and see. They take us deeply in the direction where our hearts yearn to go, but our rational minds fear to travel.

The beautiful, shifting colors in our dreams, then, are really *our* colors dancing. The frightening, amorphous beasts that rise up out of dark pools are actually *our* unknown aspects, whose gifts have not yet been revealed. And the soft, exotic melodies lightly dancing on the dream wind are really *our* inner melodies, the sounds of our own beings playing gently.

Dream images help us to remember ourselves bit by bit. They move us along on the path toward knowing and appreciating who we really are.

4. Why don't I remember my dreams?

We forget our dreams because, on some level, we choose to let our memory of them fade. Yet we may not be aware that we are making this choice.

Many times we forget our dreams because we are unfamiliar with their hidden value. Just as we pass by trees, roads, and faces during the day and forget them, so we also pass by dreams and let many of them fade beyond recall. This doesn't mean that our dreams don't exist. It just means that we filter them from memory because we don't think they have any meaning for us.

At other times, we may tell ourselves we value our dreams and would like to remember them, but still we lose our hold on them. This often occurs because we don't allow ourselves time in the morning to absorb our dreams. When we return to an intense focus on our daily work and activities as soon as we awaken, we don't leave enough room in our waking awareness for our dreams to enter in.

If you are not recalling your dreams and would like to begin doing so, I suggest that you spend some time going over the next chapter in this book. You might also try asking yourself, "Why haven't I chosen to remember my dreams?"

Then remind yourself that your dreams will only *enhance your existence,* not threaten you in any way. Dreams come from a large, loving part of you. They simply show you aspects of yourself that need to be embraced and allowed to grow.

5. Are all the beings I meet in my dreams parts of me?

Yes, all the beings in our dreams do reflect parts of ourselves. Yet this may not always be easy to see.

Sometimes we strongly resist our dream beings and immediately reject any thoughts of affiliation with them out of distrust or dislike. At other times, we just feel unfamiliar with them and don't see how we could possibly have any link to them at all.

When this happens, we must breathe deeply and relax into a peaceful, unguarded place in ourselves before we can see the ways in which these dream visitors are parts of us. Then we need to participate in some "dream adventures" with them so we can fully absorb the ways in which they mirror us.

I bumped smack into my own resistance in this area the first time I set out to teach a dream class on this topic. The night before I taught the class I had a dream about a sleazy, greasy man who ran a strip joint I'd recently seen in a movie. Oh ugh, I thought. Maybe I can tell them, "All dream beings are parts of you unless they're sleazy, greasy men who run strip joints." No, that won't do, I decided. I'll just have to explore this being and see what he has to tell me.

Boy, was I in for a surprise. When I did my first "Body and Spirit" adventure with that being, I found that I recognized the feeling of his energy in my body! Gradually I began to realize that this man's sleaziness was actually a magnified version of my own indifference to my emotions, my body, and my physical environment. This sleazy guy was teaching me to be more sensitive and caring toward myself as a human being.

As I showed myself so clearly in that situation, sometimes we have to bypass an "oh ugh" response to see the ways in which the most unlikely characters can be our teachers. And although we may not always be able to verbalize our connections with these other beings clearly, still we can explore our relationships in nonverbal ways. (See the Movement Adventures in Chapters Four and Six.)

When we are attentive, we will find parts of ourselves reflected in all sorts of other beings that cross our paths. We do not cross paths by chance either in waking life or in dreams. Even in the most quiet points of contact between ourselves and other beings, there is much to be revealed.

6. Why are dreams so bizarre?

We *think* of our dreams as "bizarre" partly because they mirror new dimensions of ourselves we haven't fully accepted yet. The huge black bear crashing through the brush, the silly person on stage in the clown suit, the ethereal blue being of the lake bathed in moon-light — all reflect parts of ourselves with which we have not yet become thoroughly familiar. As a result, the images themselves seem strange and unfamiliar, too.

The other reason we find dreams bizarre is that they play havoc with our beliefs about time and space. We like to think that an event that we experienced in Denver five years ago isn't going to reappear now in the midst of our lives in Seattle. We also like to think that the objects and people and animals that we know are going to stay pretty much the same from one moment to the next. A dog doesn't suddenly appear with the head of a fish. Buildings do not fly. But there *are* fishy dogs and airborne buildings in our dreams. Our definitions of what is possible in reality do not bind the secret, untamable parts of ourselves that appear in the dream realm.

Any time we are faced with something new that extends beyond the borders of the reality with which we are familiar, it will seem odd to us at first. Dreams are no exception. They dance right past our old self-concepts and limited ideas about time and space. We have to stretch ourselves to absorb the truths within them.

This means that if we wish to understand our dreams, we must prepare for adventure and be willing to let our dreams change the way we see things.

7. When I dream about an event happening to someone I know, is this just a symbolic message for me or am I actually dreaming about something that's going to happen to that person?

Both. First of all, a dream about something happening to someone we know is a symbolic message about the part of ourselves that that person reflects.

At the same time, a dream about someone we know shows us that our awareness is overlapping with that person's in some way. We are sensing real events within that person's experience. Yet we must remember that our dream images are *symbols* of events in that person's experience, not literal translations.

A dream about a friend of ours falling off a high diving board may not mean that that person is actually going to fall off a physical diving board. This person might, instead, trip off the porch steps or just realize that he or she is taking a big leap into a new dimension of living. Or none of the above. Interpreting our own dream images as messages about another person can be a tricky business. The only thing we can be sure of when we dream of one another is that we are stepping into each other's worlds, touching each other's experience in some way.

Perhaps the best thing to do when you dream about something happening to someone you know is to explore the dream as a symbolic message about yourself. When you have first recognized the meaning that a dream holds for you personally, then it will be easier for you to understand what this dream is telling you about someone else.

8. Why do I dream about images from my past?

We draw forth images from the past — familiar people, places, creatures, objects, and events — to remind ourselves of the inner experiences we associate with these images.

For example, if you had been chased and bitten by a big dog in your waking life when you were a child, you might draw forth this image as a dream symbol years later to speak to yourself about feelings of helplessness, fear, and pain. And if you frequently went and sat under a huge, calming tree at one time in your life, you might recall this image in your dreams years later, to remind yourself that there is a kind of serenity rooted deep within your being.

Throughout our lives, we continue to build and reshape our symbolic dream language. During this process, some images from our pasts are altered and transformed, while those that represent lasting truths about ourselves and our universe are strengthened and enlarged. These changes reflect our own shifting and growing understanding of ourselves.

9. Why do we have recurring dreams?

Dream images hold messages for us. When these messages are not getting through, or they need to be emphasized, the same images are often repeated.

Sometimes a repeating dream image is a unpleasant one. In this case, our deepest, timeless awareness has something urgent it is trying to communicate that we are not hearing. We need to participate in some dream adventures, like the ones described in this book, to understand the message an image holds before we can release the image.

At other times, our recurring images are comforting ones. We see visions of warm people and wonderful places that we never met in waking life, appearing frequently. Or we may see a person, place, or activity we *have* known and cherished, returning often in our dreams. By engaging in a "dream adventure" with these kinds of images, we help ourselves to realize that the feelings of hopefulness and tenderness these images stimulate are still available to us and are actually a vibrant, living part of ourselves.

10. Why do we have nightmares?

Usually we have nightmares when we try to forget or suppress large parts of ourselves. We get this kind of "amnesia" when we think that expressing certain parts of ourselves could interfere with our survival or with our attractiveness to others. We think parts of ourselves are ugly, dull, unruly, needy, unspiritual, unmanly, unwomanly, impractical, or completely crazy and we try and stuff them out of sight.

Yet as long as we refuse to provide the space we need in our lives to explore the true nature of our own beings, the great, dark horses of sleep will continue to appear. The apparent powers in nightmares that threaten to destroy us, to thrust something upon us we don't want, or to take something away from us we do want, are actually strong reflections of our own denial of ourselves.

Our nightmares are a signal that a deep, loving part of ourselves doesn't accept our self-rejection. It sends forth images of fear, pain, and destruction to emphasize how much we hurt ourselves by denying who we are.

When we can begin to accept and love ourselves more, our nightmares diminish. One concrete step in this direction is to remind ourselves to listen to our feelings when we are awake and not feeling scared. Then, when we are faced with an event that does frighten us, like those that appear in nightmares, we will feel more confident about expressing ourselves and can begin to recover some of our own power in those situations.

I experienced these kinds of results quite clearly, after I'd made an agreement with myself during my waking hours to start listening to my feelings more. I dreamed that a man had me pinned face down and was attacking me from behind, but I turned and yelled at him, "You're hurting me!" "I am?" he asked sheepishly. Then he got up and moved away. That dream ended a series of dreams in which dark, scary men pursued me.

Another way to begin releasing our nightmares can be to explore the images while we're awake using either Dialoguing on page 49 or Expanded Self Writing on page 112. Once we can absorb the messages in our frightening dreams there will be no need for them to reoccur.

I realize that the process of exploring our nightmares and the shadows that stretch across our days can be one of the most demanding dream journeys we participate in. This kind of a dream journey requires self-honesty and courage (not to mention love and support). Yet when we can explore our nightmares we can use this process itself to rediscover the powerful love and self-acceptance that we are capable of feeling.

11. Can I increase my psychic awareness by exploring my dreams?

Yes. When you open up psychically, you learn to look deeply at what is taking place both in and around you. Your awareness spreads out in time and space. Frequently you can uncover information about events that may be happening in other places, or that may occur in the future.

Exploring your dreams helps you to develop these abilities. As you examine your dream images and discover the emotions, beliefs, yearnings, thoughts, and inspirations that created these images, you learn to look below the surface of events. As you recognize more and more images in your dreams that reflect events happening in other places and times (including precognitive dream images that hint at future waking life events), you begin to release limiting beliefs about the paths your own consciousness can travel in time and space.

Thus, you develop your psychic awareness in a very unselfconscious way when you explore your dreams. You cultivate a certain perceptiveness that naturally extends to other areas of your life through time.

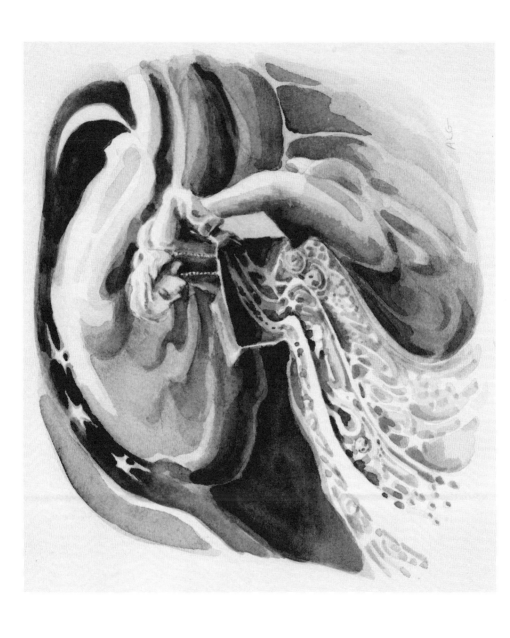

12. Do dreams affect my life?

Yes. Our dreams always affect our lives, even if we don't pay attention to them. They just touch us in a more limited, hidden way when we ignore them than they would if we gave them our full attention.

Our dreams have this affect because they help us to release the narrow focus on structures and events with which we fill our waking hours. This release, whether we remember it or not, is like the release of a heavy burden. It provides us with a sense of relief and renewal and gives us the freedom to see relationships between events and beings that are unrestricted by time and space. We *need* this freedom so that the way we see ourselves and our world can grow.

When we actively remember our dreams and explore them, we can increase the positive effect they have. Information we learned about ourselves and our world while we were asleep becomes more accessible to our conscious minds. Dream messages that offer resolutions to problems and illuminate new creative options become more available to us. We learn to use our dreams as tools for expanding our thinking and making changes in our waking lives. Thus, our dreams always affect us, but the degree to which they do depends on us and the choices we make.

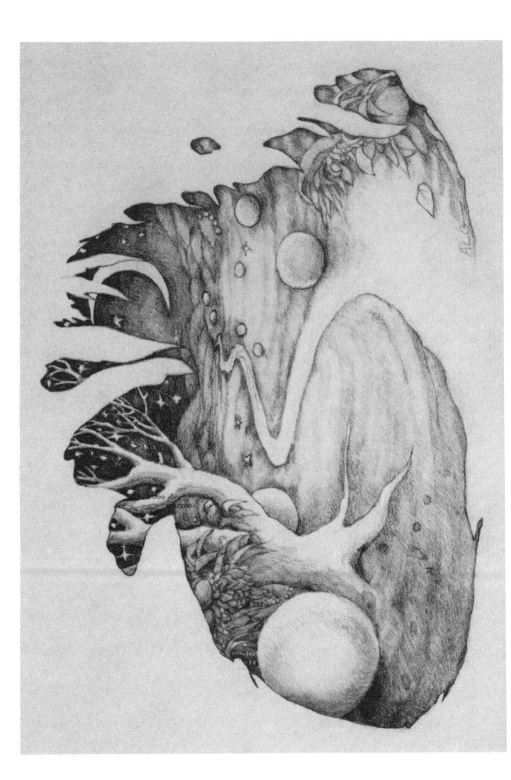

2

Welcoming, Recalling, and Recording

Your dreams are messages from your own spirit. They are waiting to be welcomed into your life. Yet many of us have trouble bringing our dreams into our lives because we have overlooked one vital aspect of welcoming them in. It is the same aspect we often overlook in some of our relationships with other people. We think we can go through the mechanics of welcoming — of opening doors, of saying "yes, I want this relationship in my life" — without also opening our hearts, minds, and bodies and embracing that relationship and the new life it brings us.

Relationships require our embrace. They require our willingness to make contact and to be transformed by that contact.

So it is with our relationship with our dreams. I can offer you all kinds of suggestions and techniques for improving your ability to recall and record your dreams but unless you are willing to open up and respond to your dreams, allowing them into your life in a full, real way, nothing I can say can help you bring your dreams to life. You must leave space and time so that the mystery and magic of dreams can become a part of your life . . . and you must move past your own fears about what they might have to tell you, so that you don't try to filter them or hold them at arm's length. Then your dreams will appear increasingly clear and meaningful to you. Your dream journey will begin all by itself.

Now I know you may feel a little foggy at this point about ways in which to welcome your dreams, especially if you have very little recall of them. Yet this chapter can guide you through this process. I invite you to read it, reflect upon it, and allow it to help you gently open to your dreams' embrace.

Before You Go to Sleep

Your Attitude Toward Dreaming

The first step toward increasing your dream recall is to examine your attitude toward dreaming. Often we place the primary emphasis in our lives on those activities which seem the most tangible — like our work, or the needs of others, or what kind of bread we should buy to eat with the lasagna. To allow ourselves the delight of paying attention to our dreams, we must shift our priorities a little. We must consider the fact that discovering more of ourselves is an activity that is at least as valuable as any other activity we might do, however intangible it may seem.

A Willingness to See New Parts of Yourself

In order to remember our dreams, we must be willing to see new parts of ourselves. If we are afraid of ourselves, we may cut off not only our understanding of dreams, but also our memory of them. If you feel drawn to your dreams, but also reluctant to recover them, you might do affirmations at night before you go to sleep. Try saying to yourself, "I am fully able to remember my dreams now," or "I look forward to discovering deeper aspects of myself, through my dreams" (or something along those lines). The main idea here is to communicate to yourself that remembering your dreams is a precious event and that your true nature, which does become more visible in dreams, is a good one.

Asking Specific Questions

Before you go to sleep, formulate in your mind a question to ask your dream self. Consider carefully what you wish to know. When the question you ask involves one or more underlying issues, the dreams that follow will reflect this.

Now write the question down and leave a notebook, sketchbook, or other recording device at your bedside to record your dreams' response to the question. When you awaken, look through your dreams carefully. The answer you find there may be symbolic, rather than direct and simple, and it may not be the kind of answer you anticipated.

Once I asked my dream self, "What work should I be doing now?" What I really wanted to know was what kind of job I should seek. However, I repeated that question to myself for three nights and for three nights I dreamed about different relationships in my life. It took some time for me to realize that the answer to my question was that my present "work" was to focus on the relationships in my life. The answer I received was so far outside the framework of the answer I expected that I didn't think I was receiving an answer!

So remember, you may need to examine your dreams very closely the morning after you have asked your dreaming self a question. The response to your question may be subtle and quite different from what you expected to hear!

Your Body

The strongest factors in dream recall have to do with your attitudes towards yourself, the value you place on dreams, and your willingness to restructure your life so that it facilitates the recall process. (I will describe this latter factor more fully in the next section in this chapter.) However, what you do with your body does affect your memory of dreams, so let's consider the affect of different eating, sleeping, and drug habits. As you read these ideas, remember that there are no hard and fast rules in this area. You will have to experiment to some degree to find what works the best for you.

Eating Habits

It is midnight. You have been staying up late with a friend, drinking a beer and eating a giant pizza smothered with Canadian bacon, black olives, and anchovies. After a good belch, you nestle down in your bed and prepare to go to sleep. Many people would claim that eating something like this right before you go to sleep might make it more difficult to remember your dreams. I have found that this is often true. Some, however, claim that dreams created on a full stomach are worthless, that they are strictly a reaction to the food you are digesting. I disagree with this claim.

Dreams hold messages for your being on many levels. All dreams can be read in terms of their meaning for your body, as well as for your emotional, mental, and spiritual growth.

What you eat does affect your dreams, but it does not cause you to have meaningless dreams that are simply a by-product of what you ate.

Hours You Sleep

When I first became very interested in remembering my dreams, I experimented with the hours I slept, by following a suggestion from *The Nature of Personal Reality* by Jane Roberts. Seth, the channeled entity who gives the information in that book, suggested that his readers try sleeping 4-6 hours at a stretch and then adding a 1-2 hour nap later in the day if needed. I tried this and found that I had some difficulty waking up after 4-6 hours; sleeping longer was so ingrained. Yet when I was able to do it, I had several amazing dream experiences, including some lucid dreams (in which I became aware that I was dreaming while I was dreaming). I also found that I remembered my dreams more clearly upon awakening and that my dreaming and waking states began to feel more integrated, just as Seth suggested they might. So, if you are interested in enhancing your dreaming (and waking) experiences, I suggest that you try this.

Sleep Companions

Your dream experiences may also be affected by the person with whom you sleep. If you feel close to that person, your dreams may become intertwined and you may both recall similar dream images when you wake up. If you are sleeping with a child or an adult whose needs are the primary focus of your waking hours, your recall of your own dreams may be hazy upon awakening. Likewise, if you feel uncomfortable about the person with whom you are sleeping, you may find it more difficult to remember your dreams when you wake up, because this person's presence may cause you to invalidate your own inner experiences.

Sleep Environment

Another influence on your dreams is the environment in which you sleep. Just as different environments may stimulate different memories and emotions in you when you are awake, so they may also trigger different types of dream images for you when you sleep. The dreams that you have when you sleep in a canyon may be a little different than the dreams you have when you lie on the beach, under the stars. And the dreams that you have on the beach will probably be a little different than those you have when snuggled warmly in your own bed. Once again, you need to experiment with these circumstances and see what happens if you wish to produce changes in your dream patterns.

Drug Habits

Another physical factor that affects dreams is the intake of drugs. Ingesting a lot of drugs, just like ingesting a lot of food before sleeping, can detract from your ability to recollect and absorb dream images. People I've known who have taken prescriptive drugs or smoked marijuana every day for long periods of time, report a decrease in their ability to remember dreams during that time and an increase after they'd stopped using the drugs for awhile. Others I know have reported that drinking alcohol in regular, large amounts has the same sort of diminishing effect on dream recall. However, I have also found that drinking coffee or alcohol in small amounts before sleeping can often help with dream recall. Once again, you will need to discover for yourself what works best for you.

After You Wake Up

Transitioning

The single most important factor in recalling dreams, next to a strong desire to do so, is giving ourselves transition time when we wake up in the morning. Many of us wake up to the sound of a shrill alarm, jump out of bed, grab our clothes, drink some coffee, and barrel out into the world — all in a matter or minutes. Later we wonder why we don't remember our dreams. We throw ourselves from the soft, fluid dream world into a waking world of precise definitions, time schedules, and "to do" lists in a very short period of time. Such a quick switch demands a great deal of energy and concentration and can be quite a shock. We leave ourselves with little energy for remembering our dreams this way.

I suggest a less shocking way of waking up if you wish to recall your dreams. Be aware of the fact that you are making a big transition when you move from an expanded, dream state of awareness to a more focused, physical state of awareness. Let this experience be as gentle as possible. If you need to wake up at a certain time, tell yourself the night before, "I will wake up at 6:30 tomorrow morning," rather than using an alarm. Then make sure that you wake up well before the time you actually have to get out of bed.

When you do awaken, stay in the original position in which you were sleeping, if you can. This will often help you to recall dream images. If you have to get up right away for any reason, try to move slowly and get back into your original sleeping position when you return to bed.

Lastly, don't try to force yourself to remember all the details of the dreams you've just experienced. Instead, allow yourself to focus on whatever images volunteer themselves. The more gentle you are with yourself as you wake up and try to remember your dreams, the more rewarding the whole process will be.

Listening to the Little Bits

Pay attention to feelings, fleeting impressions, and partially remembered pieces of dreams, especially at the beginning. Learning to converse with your dream self is like developing a dialogue with another person. By showing your willingness to listen and to absorb the content of what your dream self is saying, you encourage it to talk to you. Even when you don't like a certain image that is presented, or feel sure that it is mundane and useless, try to remain open to the possibility that there is actually a deeper message within this image that you have not yet perceived.

You will maintain a good relationship with your dreams with steady recall, when you build trust with your dream self. Show this newly discovered aspect of yourself that you are listening and it will speak back to you. The more you listen, the more you will hear. Allow the lines of communication to open within yourself.

Anchoring

After you have made the gentle transition from immersing yourself in the dream state to awakening and savoring your dream images, anchor these images in physical reality. Anchoring a dream image can mean recording it in a notebook, doing a sketch of it in a sketch pad, composing a series of sounds or movements to convey the feelings of the dream, recording the dream on a tape recorder, sharing the dream verbally with someone close to you, exploring it through one of the dream adventures in this book, or carrying out some action in your waking life that you saw taking place in your dreams.

When you are engaged in any of these ways of anchoring, you may find that other dream images that you did not remember at first, suddenly come flooding back. Anchoring is a powerful way to strengthen your recall, absorption, and understanding of dream images. Your dreams will also start to become a more real, tangible part of your life. Its importance in reinforcing the link between you and your dreams cannot be overstated.

Summary

Once again, you may need to try some of the new ways of thinking and acting described in this chapter, if you wish to remember your dreams more clearly. Yet there are no exact prescriptions for 100% dream recall. You must playfully experiment to discover what kinds of approaches work best for you.

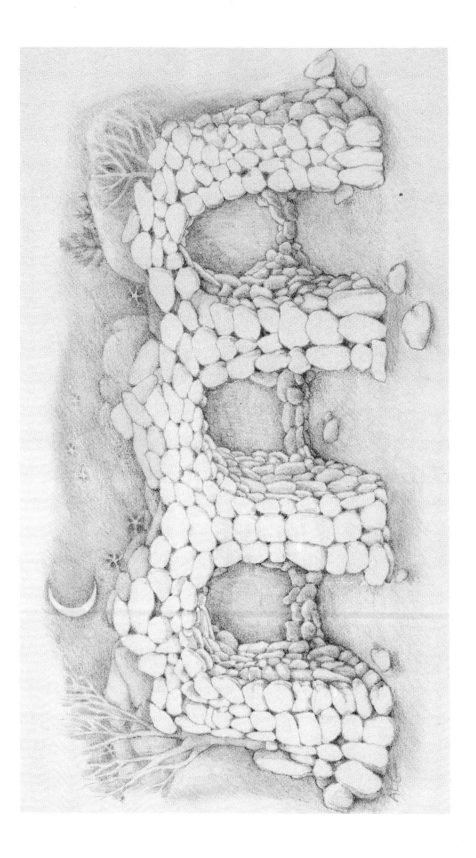

3

Secrets for a Magical Dream Journey

No field as magical as dream exploration exists without a few secrets of the trade to help that magic come alive. Some of the "secrets" described in this chapter include terms you will need to understand and materials and supplies you will need to gather before engaging in the adventures in this book. Others are guidelines for developing both an inner perspective and an outer environment that are most conducive to dream adventures. I think you will find that all of them are both easy to read over and a vibrant part of your dream journey.

Terms

Dream Character

When you engage in any dream adventure in this book, you will need to choose one dream character to explore (unless otherwise noted). A character is any image within the dream you can clearly identify — one that isn't too vague or anonymous. You should either be able to distinguish it by name, by delineating specific characteristics it has, or by describing the feelings it arouses in you.

The dream character you choose could be a person, but it doesn't have to be. You could instead choose a green vase, an old oak tree, a street called Airport Road, a heavy snowstorm, a house in which you lived as a child, etc. Any image that leaves a strong impression on you will work.

You, yourself, are often one of the characters in your dreams. However, I don't recommend that you work with yourself in these adventures. I say this because our dream explorations often get muddled when we focus directly on "ourselves." We usually give ourselves more latitude to make new discoveries when we focus on "other" dream characters instead.

Beyond this, I don't have any special formula for choosing one character over another. Sometimes you will feel a definite impulse to explore one particular character. When this happens, by all means, follow your intuition and explore that character! When you don't feel any impulses, however, just choose a character that interests you.

All characters give you information about yourself. If you explore any one on a deep level, usually the meaning behind some of the other characters and events in the dream will become clear as well. However, when you are first beginning your dream journey, I recommend that you engage in "adventures" with at least two or three different characters from one dream. This will help deepen your insight into each dream.

Dream Scene

In some of the adventures in this book, you will be asked to work with "a scene" rather than "a character." A scene can be loosely described as the part of your dream that takes place within one setting. For instance, in one scene from a dream, you and a lot of people dressed in colorful clothes might be dancing in a meadow. Suddenly the dance gets interrupted by a troop of badgers who are marching double file, right through your dancing area. You and the other people stand back in wonder. In this case, the meadow, the people dancing, the colorful clothes, the troop of marching badgers, and the feeling of wonder — are all aspects of the same scene. The scene is the whole picture that includes events, characters, objects, and feelings or moods.

There are no rules to follow in selecting which scene to explore in a dream adventure. Just pick the scene that intrigues you the most.

Materials and Supplies

For all writing adventures, you will need a pen and paper. For all art adventures and adventures with children, you will need an "art box." An art box is a box full of knickknacks and other materials that could be used in art projects. The art box I use in my classes contains magazines, construction paper, crayons, markers, pens, paints, brushes, glitter, glue, scissors, play dough, feathers, buttons, lace, foil, popsicle sticks, wrapping paper, stick-on stars, sequins, clothespins, toilet paper rolls, small boxes, felt, crepe paper, cotton balls, hangers, twigs, stones, straw flowers, and little shells (among other things). If you are exploring a dream journey with a group of people, each member of the group can bring in one or two items for a collective art box. That way each one of you will have a bigger variety of materials to explore.

For movement, meditation, and verbal adventures you need just curiosity, patience, and imagination.

A Quiet Place and Time

The best place to practice dream adventures is a quiet, private place without a lot of distractions where you can listen to yourself. Sometimes the best way to create this is to establish a little sanctuary — one special place in your house where you always return when you want to explore your dreams.

The best time for embarking on dream adventures is a period of the day when you don't feel hurried and you feel drawn to exploring your dreams. I recommend that you act on the impulse to explore your dreams as much as you can and that you be aware of the time of day that is generally easiest for you to absorb dream adventures.

For me, this time is usually in the morning, immediately after I've recorded my dreams. However, you might find that a different time works best for you.

Relaxation

When you explore any one of your dreams in detail, you are speaking to yourself on a deep level. And it's much easier to converse with yourself on a deep level when you relax! The following simple breath and movement exercise can assist you with this.

Preparation

Ask someone to read the following text to you slowly, or read it aloud yourself, tape it, and play it back when you are ready to enter this adventure. This way, you can just release all other thoughts and surrender to the experience.

Adventure

Sit or lie down in a comfortable position and close your eyes.

Gradually become aware of your breath . . . Feel the way your breath pushes against your clothes . . .

Notice how your breath rises and falls. Let it rise as fully as it wants to and fall as fully as it wants to . . .

Follow your breath as if you were riding a wave . . . Each time that you inhale, imagine yourself rising up on the crest of a wave. And each time that you exhale, imagine yourself sliding down the other side of the wave.

Continue this for five more breaths, letting yourself relax more each time you breathe . . .

Then open your hands, turn them palm upwards, and place them on your thighs (or on the floor, if you are lying down). Breathe in and slowly close your hands . . . Breathe out and slowly open your hands . . .

Each time that you breathe in, feel your own strength. Each time that you breathe out, allow yourself to open up to parts of the universe with which you aren't yet acquainted.

Repeat these movements at least five times. Breathe fully, in an unhurried way, and move your hands slowly each time.

After you have done this, feel the energy in your hands . . . Allow your hands to relax . . . Allow your whole body to relax . . .

As your body relaxes, let a feeling of peacefulness spread throughout your whole being. Allow yourself to be at peace with yourself . . . Notice how this feels . . .

Now let your feelings expand with each breath . . .

Continue the process of breathing and expanding for a little while.

Now prepare to end this meditation. In a moment, you will open your eyes and begin a dream adventure. When you do so, remember to give yourself the time and space you need to stay in touch with the feelings and the wisdom inside you.

Breathe deeply once again. Now open your eyes and softly return your attention to the physical world. Take as much time as you need to make this a gentle transition. Then prepare to engage in one of the dream adventures found in the next chapter.

Resistance

Every one of us has moments when we experience resistance. On the dream journey, our resistance usually appears when we're trying to get in touch with the feelings associated with a certain dream character. We try to explore a character and we don't get very far. We feel numb, foggy, distracted, unusually tired, or frustrated and annoyed.

Many times, if we're just patient with ourselves and relax when this happens, we can dissolve our own resistance enough to move through it. Yet at other moments, relaxation just doesn't seem to dissipate the resistance. We breathe, relax, and wait, but the situation doesn't change.

At these times, we need to explore the resistance itself. We need to talk to it — to find out why it's there, what it has to tell us, what it's trying to protect us from.

To do this, I recommend that you personify your resistance. Imagine a character that reflects your resistant feelings — like a foggy field, a big, black bull, a brick wall, or a little boy throwing tantrums. Once you've found this character, turn to the Dialoguing adventure on page 49, and converse with the character. Dialogue with your resistance character until you begin to understand the fear that created it. What was it you were afraid to feel or know when you explored your dream? Ask it to suggest ways that you could diminish this fear.

Then remember these guidelines in the future, if ever your own resistance trips you up once again. We all hit walls from time to time on our dream journey, whether we're just beginning to explore dreams or whether we've been exploring them for some time. Learn to turn the situation around and make it work for you.

Practice and Patience

I never used to like the word "practice" at all, thinking it was a word that only piano teachers used. "Playing" always sounded more fun than "practicing" did to me.

Yet as I've gotten older, I've begun to realize that many forms of joy do take some sort of regular attention before they can blossom. Opening up to yourself takes time. Becoming quiet enough inside so that you can make contact with your own inner wisdom during a dream adventure takes practice.

The more gentle and persistent we are on our dream journey, the more it will touch us, the more profound the results of the adventures will be. Over the years, I have watched many of my students who were totally baffled by their dreams at first discover all kinds of insights from their dreams. I have also seen my own understanding of myself, my world, and my dreams grow tremendously as a result of continued attention to my dreams.

I know that when we are willing to be patient with ourselves and practice exploring our dreams on a regular basis, our ability to understand them does deepen in time. We learn how to speak with our dreams and they become our teachers.

4

Basic Dream Adventures

Before you begin this chapter, make sure you familiarize yourself with Chapter Three. It contains vital information you will need for your dream journey, such as the definition of a "dream character" and a list of the materials you will use.

In this chapter, you will find some of the most simple and straightforward dream adventures I know. These adventures are divided into writing, art, meditation, and movement sections (with examples of my own included in the writing section). You can work with them in any order, or you can follow the guidelines in the Eight-Day Dream Journey, beginning on page 74.

The most important thought to keep in mind as you begin these adventures is to keep a relaxed and playful attitude about what you're doing. If you were in one of my workshops, I'd rant and rave and say silly things to remind you that exploring your dreams is a magical, adventurous process, not a grim, analytical business. Since I can't stand in front of you and say this, however, I would like to remind you now that there will be no right or wrong answers in your findings. Let go of your concern about finding the right answers. Savor these adventures instead. Enter into them with the intent to enhance your life, to open up new doors, and gaze off into new vistas. Then allow your dream understanding to deepen gradually.

At the same time, remember that you don't have to consider yourself a writer to scribble words on paper, an artist to express yourself through color and texture, a Buddhist monk to be quiet and listen deeply to yourself, or a dancer to experience simple new positions and movements with your body. These adventures are experiments designed to help you discover new insights into your dreams. Let yourself do new things. This will help you to see new things.

A part of reclaiming your own dreams is reclaiming your own creativity. Reawaken the innocence in you that lets you know it's okay to be creative — to be playful, to enjoy your own growth, and to express yourself without restraint. Then get out your crayons, your pencils, your paper, and your dancing shoes. The door to your dreams lies open.

❧ *Writing* ❧

Free Association Writing

In this adventure, you allow your mind to flow from one image to another in a stream of consciousness. Sometimes when I participate in this adventure, I feel as though I am standing in a thick mist, seeing only the vague outline of the dream's shape before me. I use my writing to help me move towards that shape, to clarify what my senses, emotions, and memories are telling me about it. I focus on a dream character and then respond to it with my whole being. In this way, some aspect of my inner awareness becomes more alive, and I start to feel more alive, too. I give sanction to an unacknowledged part of myself that wishes to speak and be heard.

Adventure

Begin to record your impressions of your dream character on paper. Write down how this character makes you feel and what this character reminds you of. If other dream, memory, and fantasy images come to mind as you contemplate this character, explore your feelings about them, too. Examine your character's relationship to these images.

Write without pausing. If you start to get stuck, just repeat the last word you wrote down or write "um, um, um . . ." until your flow of expression gets going again.

The more freely you write, the more information you will uncover. You don't have to write in elegant sentences or even whole ones. You don't have to think in a highly structured way about your inner images. Just use your writing as a tool to help you clarify your feelings about the character.

The main purpose of this adventure is to write about what you feel. Allow yourself to describe your feelings rather than interpret the images with your intellect. In this way, you will be more sensitive to your dream character and you will find that it naturally reveals its message to you as you write about it.

You may find the following questions to be of assistance in this process. I don't recommend using them, however, if they seem to slow down the flow of your writing.

- How does this character feel to you?

- What do your senses tell you about this character? Can you describe the character using colors, sounds, shapes, smells, textures, and qualities of light?

- What does this character remind you of? Does it remind you of anything you've been experiencing recently in your waking life?

- Does this character bring up any fears for you?

- Does this character inspire you in any way?

Note: If you feel that the character with which you are free-associating is a negative one, and participating in this adventure just increases your own feelings of doubt and negativity, try free-associating on the question "How is this character a part of me that's trying to grow?" "Negative characters" just reflect parts of us that have more to learn. We need to see a character we think of as "negative" as a symbol of one phase of our growth process. Then we can help this part of ourselves transform into something positive. If the character you have chosen to explore is one that you recognize from waking life but that is portrayed differently in the dream, turn to the Waking/Dream Free Association adventure on page 102 and follow that adventure in place of this one.

Dream Log

In this dream I am running away from someone. Eventually I know I will return and face this person. At this moment, however, an uncontrollable desire to run, to escape, and to be free is welling up in me.

During my attempt to escape, I come to a platform that wraps around a long pipe. Behind the pipe is an arched wooden door held closed by a hook and latch. I step onto the platform to go out through the door. The platform bends a little under my weight.

Once I have passed through the door, I have to fumble with the hook to try and close the door. I can't latch it again very easily. I start to go without getting it securely latched. Then I stop and wonder — what if someone else comes this way? It seems to me that the hook and the latch actually hold the platform together and if I don't get the hook well fastened I might be endangering the life of anyone who tries to step on the platform.

With these thoughts in mind, I go back and fumble with the latch until I think it's at least adequately fastened. Then I leave.

Free Association (On the Platform Area)

This is a dark, old place. It reminds me of an attic . . . a place up high that's just right for a child to hide in and imagine great secrets. When I was little, I wanted so much to find a place like this. A place where I could hide, undiscovered . . . where I could revolve inside without comment from others or justification to them . . . where I could find an exit if I needed to . . . Here, as an adult in this dream, I find that place I once yearned for.

I come across this place when I am barreling forward towards my own freedom. Feeling an impulse to break out, to go outside, to somehow eject into a world of the imagination, I end up at this platform area, with its door to another world. I am trying to protect my own beauty and creativity by coming here, I think. Yet I am also trying to escape.

When I was a child, escape and freedom meant the same thing to me. If I could find a way to escape from the restrictions and narrow expectations I encountered in my daily life, I felt free. But now, my weight presses on the platform. I am no longer a child and freedom does not mean the same thing to me that it did then.

I realize this when I have to fumble with the hook and latch on the door. Having to deal with the hook and latch helps me bring my awareness back to the reality of what I'm doing, back to the reality of the present moment. As I am forced to pause in my running I begin to realize that my freedom no longer lies in separating myself and my experience from other beings. A very real part of me now is drawn into a communion with others. I feel a deep sense of unity with sky and trees and human beings that I can no longer shake off.

For this reason I can't just keep running. I can't fly from this world like a single, isolated bullet hurtling through space. I am coming to a time in my life when I will have to turn to face this truth instead — that my freedom is found in expressing my beauty and creativity in my daily life here on earth.

Rewording

This adventure contains a step by step technique, for those of you who learn best by having each individual step of a process clearly delineated. Those of you who learn more easily when you can sense the steps in a process intuitively may trip over your own feet in this adventure, but try it anyway! Knowing how to free-associate on dream characters and reword your description of them is a fundamental tool for all dream journeys.

Adventure

1. Free-associate on your dream character. (Write down any feelings, sensation, messages, or images that come to your mind in response to this character.)

2. Now write down what part of you this character represents.

3. In just a few sentences, describe the events in which this character was involved in the dream. Be careful not to get much longer than three sentences, or this adventure will become too complex.

4. Underline any nouns in these sentences and any verbs or adjectives that seem unusual or interesting to you.

5. Make a separate list of these words.

6. Free-associate briefly on each one. Record your strongest impressions of each.

7. Now you are going to reword the situation you have described in three sentences. First you need to replace the name of your main character with the brief description of the part of you that character represents (that you came up with in step 2).

8. Then you need to replace the words you underlined with your free associations for each of those words.

9. Now loosely reword the situation, describing it as an inner event, involving part of you.

Dream Log 1

Dream character: a pond.

1. Pond: a calm, tranquil, serene place. Round, smooth, quiet, peaceful.

2. Part of myself the pond represents: A peaceful state of awareness within myself, how I'm feeling when I'm relaxed.

3 & 4. In this dream, I am hanging around a <u>pond</u>, looking at <u>plants</u> in the pond. I am learning about <u>animals</u> that are harmful to the plants and ones that are not. <u>Slugs</u> are not. <u>Small bugs with black backs</u> are. They eat the plants.

5 & 6. Plants: growth, confidence, hope.

Animals: life forms that move, creatures.

Slugs: creatures that move slowly.

Small bugs with black backs: animals with darkness behind them, worries about darkness, gnawing fears from the past.

7-9. Rewording: Within me is a calm, tranquil place in which growth is occurring. While I am focused on this calm, tranquil place, I learn that moving slowly is not harmful to my growth. Feelings of darkness in my past do gnaw away at me, however, and can be harmful to my growth.

Dream Log 2

Dream character: a herd of cows.

1. Cows: heavy, earthy animals. Slow-witted, docile. Their lives are made up of their physical functions . . . eating, sleeping, expelling, giving milk, giving birth. Usually they are kept in a herd and they take directions from humans.

2. Part of myself the cows represent: The part of me that feels heavy, earthbound, and kind of slow-witted sometimes. The part of me that forgets my spirit in flight and tells myself, "I am my physical body. I am my emotions. And that is all I am. I don't know what to do with myself. I need someone else to lead me."

3 & 4. In this dream, it's <u>dark</u> and I figure it's time to move <u>the cows</u> from <u>one pasture</u> to another. I call for help from <u>my mother</u>, but don't get any. I realize <u>I</u> must be totally responsible for doing this on my own.

5 & 6. Dark: the unknown . . . the end of one day, one phase. The unclear time before a new phase begins.

Pasture: a place where cows hang out, carrying out their life functions. An area, a field.

My mother: a loving, nurturing being who often makes decisions based on her intellectual analysis of a situation.

I: an unfolding being who wants to rely on other parts of my awareness, besides my intellect, for guidance in decision-making.

7-9. Rewording: It's the time of the unknown, when one phase has ended and another has not yet begun. I feel I need to shift my focus into a new area now, yet I feel heavy and slow-witted, as if I can't figure out for myself what to do next. I don't think I know how to move my life in a new direction unless I appeal to my intellect. But I find that this part of myself doesn't help me. Gradually I realize that I must face the changes I need to make in my life as the unique, unfolding being I truly am. I must love myself and trust my own inner wisdom to help me, in unexpected ways, to find the new areas of focus that I seek.

Point of View

When you enter into this adventure, you will experience a dream from a dream character's point of view. By examining the dream from this new perspective, your own awareness of that dream can expand. You will be able to see things about the dream that you did not notice when you were just looking at it from your own point of view.

I believe that tribal cultures benefited a great deal from rituals in which they took on the perspective of another being — becoming a tree, a snake, a wind spirit. We, in this fast-paced, technological world, often keep our individual boundaries so firm that we miss the experience of truly being one with another being. Because I know that this kind of practice is not encouraged in our culture, I ask you to be patient with yourself as you move through this adventure. And I encourage you to keep experimenting with it until it really works for you — until you can fully release the barriers between yourself and a dream being.

Adventure

Like a child "pretending," imagine that you *are* your dream character. Keep your new identity throughout the whole dream adventure and stay focused on this character's point of view.

Look through this character's eyes and write down the entire dream from this new perspective. Use the personal pronoun "I" when speaking as this character.

Record all that you see and feel as this character. Also pay particular attention to anything that you see as this character that you didn't see from your original point of view in the dream. Notice too, the way in which you, as this character, see "you, the dreamer" within the dream.

Dream Log

I am a helper of some sort in a well-to-do household. The woman who has been giving me instructions about taking care of the plants upstairs, tells me that soon her husband will be bringing their son and some of their son's friends home for a party. They'll be drinking in the kitchen.

My bedroom is right by the kitchen, so even though their son is fairly clean-cut and probably not rowdy, I feel regret that the party is taking place. I go into the kitchen to see what the boys will be drinking and I find bottles of Pinot Noir on ice.

Point of View Adventure (Perspective of Bottle of Pinot Noir)

Mmmmm. I am a bottle of red wine. Rich and exquisite, I exist for highly cultured people. I live for the pleasure of those who can recognize the distinction between things of quality and things without quality.

I am a little snobby, impressed by myself, I would say. I don't want to be opened up unless someone is really going to appreciate me and savor me. I wouldn't be so snobby if everyone had that ability. But my artfulness and the joy I offer do not really come forth until people take the time to smell me, taste me, and get to know me. I love to be savored.

Now this family has bought me as one of many bottles for their teenage son's party. I'm not thrilled about this. I'm apt to be gulped down and that is not my style. I'd rather stay in my bottle! (Even though fulfillment for me really comes through people drinking me.) This family knows that I am expensive and said to be good. But they just get me along with all these other bottles and really don't focus on me. They take me for granted. They put me on ice and *I don't go on ice!* I am meant to be warmed in the room. I need to be warm and breathing before I can open my heart and let my robust flavor come forth.

Now Ana Lora comes to me and holds me in her hands. She notices my lovely name, "Pinot Noir," and she sees my little label — the one with the picture of the vineyards on it. It sets her to dreaming of Europe and fine experiences that she wishes she could have . . . that she thinks only come to people with a lot of money.

I certainly prefer her touch to the experience of being tossed in the bucket for Junior's party (and served on ice). She sees me as an individual. She takes me in. She appreciates me. I would love it if she felt she could have me . . . if she would gather some friends around one evening in a warm kitchen and share me with them.

But she doesn't. She puts me aside for now, feeling that I belong to someone else and that I will only be hers to hold in a future she cannot yet perceive. I want to tell her that she short-changes herself. She needs to open herself to the fullness within her *now* . . . and this fullness will be reflected back to her, whether she has a lot of money or not.

Dialoguing

If there is one dream adventure for you to learn, it is this one. You could call this adventure the grandmother or granddaddy of all dream adventures. Psychologists refer to the verbal form of this adventure as "gestalt work." Psychics call it "channeling." Children call it "let's pretend." Somewhere along the way, I started calling it "dialoguing." Whichever name you use, this is one of the most direct and powerful dream adventures you can enter into. I recommend that you practice it often and use it frequently as a companion to your other dream adventures.

Preparation

In this adventure, you are going to ask your dream character some of the questions listed below. During this process you may need to remind yourself periodically to return to a state of inner stillness.

Sometimes your own self-doubt or "rational thinking" may block your ability to converse with your dream character. When this happens, just take a deep breath, find the place of quiet serenity within yourself, and ask your question again. When you receive an answer, ask yourself, "Is this the whole truth?" If it is not, take a deep breath and ask the question again.

Remember that your dreams come from within you. The wisdom to understand them is within you also. You just need to practice listening. So, be patient with yourself . . . Know that your dream channel *will* open and that your dream characters are always available to speak to you. Now, relax and allow yourself to open up to the experience of this adventure.

Adventure

Take five deep breaths. Slow down inside. Come to a warm, tranquil place within.

Now, focus on your character. When you ask a question, imagine that your character responds directly to you, using the word "I."

As soon as you start to hear your character's response to a question, begin to record this response in writing. Remember to ask as many questions as you need to. You can add any questions to the list below that you feel you need to ask.

- Who are you? How does it feel to be you?

- What do you have to teach me?

- What part of me do you represent?

- How would you like to grow inside me?

- Is there anything else you wish to tell me at this time?

When the dialogue is complete, thank your dream character, take five deep breaths, and quietly return your focus to yourself and your environment.

Dream Log 1

I was out walking with some older, strong, white-haired women who were the leaders of a group. Their role was to protect the individuals in their group and to help them stay balanced, especially during times of change. When it started to snow, we all headed back to the group. These white-haired leaders needed to be with their group whenever a time of change, like this snowfall, arrived.

As we approached, I saw members of the group walking towards us. Some of them were older women and they looked very beautiful, walking slowly and serenely in the snow.

Dialogue with the White-haired Women Leaders

Me: White-haired women, how does it feel to be you?

Women: We feel calm. We can breathe. We are not hurried. We *know.* We have cleared the distractions from our lives so that we know how to act, when to turn, and what others in our care are feeling. We lend our serenity to the world as trees do, only we are human.

Me: Why did I need to meet you in this dream?

Women: Because you need to know that we can exist in human form . . . That humans, that you, can be like the trees that you love and still be a shepherd of sorts, exerting a gentle presence and pressure in the world. Contemplating us helps to bring you into stillness.

Me: What else do you have to teach me?

Women: Let go of the things that fetter you, that which binds your spirit. Trust that you are eternal and feel the wisdom within you. Let your caring grow. Pay attention to what you do and what you are offering. Let yourself become weightless and realize that in a timeless state of awareness you can perceive the actions you need to take in your life.

Me: What part of me do you represent?

Women: A part that is very light and sensitive and gentle, and also wise and alert. We did not come to this lightness through sleep, but from alertness. Yet this alertness extends to the deepest reaches of our beings and we have listened to those far places in our own beings as a tree listens to the farthest reaches of its roots. We extend our wisdom through contemplation and graceful, clear movement. We also see change coming in as slowly as snow falls. Because we perceive it and its meaning long before others do, we are not surprised or frightened when forms change. This is the key for you. Listen to the snow falling in your being. Respond as soon as you feel the first quivers of movement. Prepare your being for what is to come. If you are to be travelling, for example, lighten your load and don your travelling clothes so that you are ready when the day of travelling actually dawns.

Me: What do you have to tell me about new ways to grow and love?

Women: Only this . . . when one feels and responds and contemplates on a deep level and is not constantly "surprised" or "tossed about" by events, there is much more room within for love. There is less worry, and more space within you so that you can feel love. As you learn this, you will also come to see and love yourself more.

Me: Thank you, lovely women.

Women: You are most welcome.

Dream Log 2

A white owl flies into my range of vision, making a beeline for a smaller bird near a tree and catching the smaller bird in its mouth. The little bird might have gotten away again, I'm not sure.

Dialogue with the Owl

Me: Owl, who are you?

Owl: I am an exquisite, magical symbol of power to you. I am strong and direct. I watch things intently, but I also have within my being the ability to let go, to be light, and to act quickly.

Me: Why do you appear to me in the form of an owl?

Owl: You have always been fascinated by owls. I am not such a common part of your existence that you would ignore me. I can remind you of the dusky moonlit nights in the woods and the way that dreams sometimes awaken and move in the darkness. Also, my eyes remind you of wisdom, because they are not afraid to look and not afraid to see.

Me: Why do you appear white to me?

Owl: In this dream, I appear white to remind you of the winter. Winter is a time of complete surrender in nature — when the world releases its old life forms in preparation for new life to come. Also, winter is going to be a powerful time for you this year in your waking life, so I come in a vision of whiteness and power to remind you of that.

Me: How does it feel to be you?

Owl: Well, I can't describe myself as an owl in comparison to something else, or as an owl separate from the rest of the universe. I feel that I have always been an owl and will always be an owl, unlike yourself who sometimes thinks that you can change your essential identity from day to day. I know that the universe and I are one. In my dreams I just become a bigger owl that catches more and more of the world in my beak. More and more of the world becomes a part of the me owl, and I become more and more a part of the world Owl with a capital O. I take joy in myself and feel the world *through* myself, and yet the world and I are one.

Me: Why do you do what you do in the dream?

Owl: I catch the little bird to show you the way that a smaller life form surrenders itself to a larger life form. This is a vision of your present self surrendering to the larger power within you that you are capable of embodying. The smaller form feeds the larger . . . I catch the little bird not to destroy it, to push it from this earth, but to eat it, to take it into myself, and to give it a new life within the larger body that is me.

Me: What part of me are you?

Owl: I am the part of you that has accepted its own strength without promoting a dislike of weakness or misjudgment. I am the part of you that you will know has devoured you when you rise up one morning and go out the door, realizing your total commitment to your inner truth. When I have eaten you into my power you will realize that no one can stop you from being you any longer. Then the impossible will become possible for you. Mistakes and obstacles will no longer slow you down. You will have given over completely to your own growth, to the moving life force within you.

Me: Thank you, old white one.

Owl: You are welcome, little one.

Themes

In this adventure, you look at your dream as a whole, examine all the images, and then find the threads that tie them together. This will give you a general idea of your dream's messages. In order to absorb these messages more fully, I suggest that you follow this adventure with Dialoguing on page 49, or Theme Free Association on page 105.

Preparation

Select a whole dream to explore, rather than a single dream character. One with multiple images in it is best.

Adventure

Look for *parallel* images within this dream — images that are similar to one another. Jot these down.

Then look for *contrasting* images in the dream — images that are "opposites" or that just don't appear to mesh with one another. Jot these down, too.

Now take a look at the relationships between the images. What are some of the key relationships within this dream? What do they remind you of? How do they make you feel? Jot down some notes on your responses to these questions.

Then see if you can write several statements describing the main threads or themes within this dream. You might also want to try making up some titles for the dream. (Sometimes it's fun to treat this adventure as a game or a puzzle. How many parallels and contrasts can you find in one dream? See which ones you can find in the dreams described below, and then compare your answers with mine.)

Dream Log 1

My friend William's parents came to check up on me. His father, a man with blond-white hair and glasses, was dressed in a suit. He struck me as an intellectual sort of person.

He wanted to question me, but his daughter led him away before he could. Later, however, we began discussing the weather in Minnesota. William's father said the sun only shone about half the time there. I said, "That's not true. Even when it snows, the sun shines there. Here it's gray all the time." I added that I wouldn't be living in northern California if it weren't for the special relationships I had with people there. I told the others who were listening that I wouldn't recommend moving to northern California. At the same time, I wondered what William would think of Minnesota.

In another scene, William and I were exploring a toy store. It was built like a playhouse. You pushed on the panels and they turned around or lowered down. I wasn't quite sure of what to do, so I let William go ahead of me. I thought it was great, however — a toy store that was built as if it were a place to play! I figured that the kids who came here probably had a great time running through these panels.

The next thing I knew, I was outside, walking somewhere alone. I saw a man standing by a big bonfire he had built. I went over to it and warmed myself, telling him I really liked "the heat."

Parallels

- In one scene I am considering the inner environment of the toy store. In another I am discussing the outer environments of Minnesota and northern California. In both of these images, then, I am "evaluating environments."

- Sun in Minnesota and the bonfire. Both of these are images of heat and sun.

- The toy store and William (a fun-loving individual, leading the way around the toy store). Both of these are images of playfulness.

Contrasts

- Between William's father (older, intellectual, stiff) and the playfulness of the toy store and William.
- Between William's father's view of the weather in Minnesota and my view of the weather there.
- Between the weather in Minnesota (snow and sun) and the weather in northern California (no snow, little sun).
- Between the harmony of the toy store (its theme, products, and environment were all reflective of one another) and the lack of harmony in my life in northern California. (I like my relationships with people there, but I don't like the weather, and I say I wouldn't recommend moving there to anyone else.)

Themes

I am considering what it means to create harmony in my life . . . where my inner intent and my external environment would be reflective of one another. I am also feeling drawn to more heat and sun. And my strictly intellectual analysis of all this (as represented by William's father) differs from my own gut-level responses.

Titles for this Dream

Love Ties Me to the Gray
My Heart Yearns for Fires
Bespectacled Intellect Sees Little Brightness
The Secret of the Unfolding Toy Store

Dream Log 2

A group of us in the woods were experimenting with healing and transporting ourselves to new dimensions through shifts in thought. I don't know the details of what happened, but I do know that what we tried did work. It felt like magic.

Next, I entered a store that sold some of the posters I designed last year. I found a little girl sitting inside a box of my posters and I pulled her out. Later, I also found a young man sitting in a box of my posters. After I explained to him why it was important to me that he get out, he climbed out, of his own accord.

Outside the store, I walked along a hallway in a red dress, tights, and shoes. I realized that I probably looked good in this outfit, but that it was probably "too young" for me in some ways. The dress was also a little tight on me.

In the next scene, I was riding my bicycle home on a wide, asphalt road. I came to a hill at one point, and found that I could make it up the slope without too much difficulty, if I just stood up to pedal. Around this time, a group of men and women my age or a little older, rode past me on bicycles. They seemed to be on some sort of tour. All of their faces reflected a certain depth and intelligence. I was very intrigued by them and thought to myself, "So . . . people like this do exist."

At the top of the hill, this group stopped to examine a large, majestic house on the right — some sort of historical site. I rested nearby, thinking about the route I would take home from here. I intended to take the biggest road — the main road — because I thought it would be the quickest way. I wondered if the tour group would be going the same way.

As I thought about this, I looked off, down the other side of the hill from the house, and saw a canal with some buildings above it. The tops of these buildings were darkly silhouetted against a glowing sky. Whether it was sunrise or sunset I was watching, I did not know. Nor did I know where I was, although the place looked like Venice to me. I imagined that that was where I was.

Parallels

- ◗ People are sitting in the boxes my posters were in and I am wearing an outfit that is too tight and too young for me. Both of these are images of limitation and restriction.

- ◗ I do "thought experiments" with the group in the woods, travel home on a wide road, power myself uphill, meet the people in the bicycle tour group who have interesting faces, arrive at the large, majestic house, and finally discover a view of Venice. All of these are images of transporting myself through positive thought into broader, richer experiences.

Contrasts

- Between the restrictiveness of sitting in a box, wearing tight clothes, and the expansiveness of the roads I took home, my experiences along the way.

Themes

Examining the way thought affects experience. Looking at my own limited ideas about the posters I designed, and at my own narrow view of myself and my potential. Discovering how more expansive, healing thoughts can bring me wonderful new encounters and inspiring visions.

Titles

Creativity Stuck in a Box
Finding the Real Promises Life Holds for Me
Venicelight in My Eyes

❧ *Art* ❧

Free Association Artwork

This is one of the simplest art adventures described in this book. It is a colorful form of free association that allows you to explore a dream character, a scene, or a whole dream in a flowing, nonverbal way.

Preparation

Gather a sketch pad or paper (any color paper will work) and some art tools like pastels or crayons, pen and ink, colored pencils, markers, watercolors, or other paints. You can use the rest of your art box, too, if you like. Select one of the following variations to this adventure, and pick either a dream character, scene, or a whole dream to explore.

Adventure

With a Dream Character

Close your eyes and quietly reflect on this character. What is the character like? How do you respond to this character? After you have contemplated these questions, open your eyes.

Now take your paper and put some patches of *colors* on it that remind you of this character.

After you have done this, put down some *shapes* that remind you of this character (circles, squares, curves, zigzags, big shapes made up of thick lines, little shapes made up of delicate lines, etc.).

Then add *textures* or other elements to the piece that remind you of this character (soft materials like cotton balls, cloth, or leather, intricate materials like cloth and wrapping paper with complex designs, shiny materials like foil, sequins, glitter, etc.).

Finally add any *drawn symbols* or images that you feel particularly represent your dream character.

When you are done, contemplate your work and see if you can begin to absorb the spirit of this character.

With a Dream Scene

Close your eyes and picture the scene. What was happening here, and how did you feel about it? What was the setting for this scene like? What kind of light, colors, shapes, textures, sounds, smells, and moods were a part of this scene?

Open your eyes and put the colors, shapes, textures, and drawn symbols or images on your paper that you think represent this scene. When you are done, contemplate your artwork. Notice what feelings it brings up in you. Let your work help you to absorb the scene itself more deeply.

With a Whole Dream

Settle into a relaxed position, close your eyes, and remember the dream. What part of the dream had the greatest impact on you? What were the strongest feelings this dream awakened in you? After you have reflected on this, open your eyes.

Now you are going to translate your feelings about the dream into visual images, in one of two ways. One approach is to draw an image that depicts those dream events that had the greatest impact on you. The other approach is to put colors, shapes, and textures on your paper that illustrate your strongest feelings about the dream. Remember to be experimental and to pay attention to your responses as you create this image.

Note: You can use any of the above three variations to this adventure as a means of recording your dreams in the morning. I like to keep a dream journal/sketch pad and some oil pastels by my bed so that I can record my dreams this way whenever I feel the impulse to do so.

Companion Adventures

From Chapter 4, *Writing:* Free Association Writing.
From Chapter 6, *Writing:* Character Description, Scene Description, or Informal Haiku.

Gifts

Most of us need to be reminded that our dream characters have something to share with us *and* that we have something to share with them. This adventure is a good one for you to participate in when you wish to understand this exchange more fully. It is an accompaniment to the Gift Exchange Meditation in the Meditation section of this chapter.

Preparation

Turn to the Gift Exchange Meditation on page 66. If you know someone who could read this meditation to you, or if you could tape this meditation and then play it back to yourself for this adventure, do so.

Adventure

Prepare for a quiet period of contemplation. Then follow the Gift Exchange Meditation. When you are done with this meditation, consider the ways in which you might create the gifts you exchanged, or symbols of these gifts, out of the materials in your art box. (If you did not receive clear images of the gifts during the meditation, do the Dialoguing adventure now, and then ask what the gifts are.)

Assemble these gifts using materials in your art box. When you are done, you might want to glue the gifts into your dream journal (if they fit), or hang them on the wall by your bed. Contemplate what these gifts mean to you.

Companion Adventures

From Chapter 4, *Writing:* Dialoguing, Point of View; *Movement:* Basic Positions, Body and Spirit; *Meditation:* Meditation with a Dream Character.

❧ *Meditation* ❧

I suggest that you either find a friend to read these meditations to you in a slow, quiet voice, or that you tape yourself reading them aloud and then play the tape back when you are ready to meditate.

Meditation with a Dream Character

In this basic adventure, you explore a dream character in a very direct way.

Adventure

> Settle into a relaxing position. Close your eyes, breathe deeply, and be at ease.
>
> Envision your dream character in front of you. After you have done this, imagine yourself walking around this character. Examine this character with all of your senses.
>
> Notice how you feel in the presence of this character . . . Then position yourself so you can gaze into the character's eyes. If this character is one that didn't have eyes in the dream, like a mountain or a chair, imagine the eyes now. What do these eyes look like? Gaze into them and let yourself feel the essence of this character — the spirit that is reflected in the eyes. Understand the deepest desire of this character.
>
> Then ask this character to present you with a musical tone that is symbolic of its spirit. Listen . . .
>
> Next, ask for a color that reflects its spirit. Watch . . .

Now ask for a symbol that represents its spirit. Watch again . . .

Absorb any other information or feelings that come to you after you have recognized the tone, the color, and the symbol.

Then imagine yourself touching this character. If this character is a person, you might want to try touching hands. As you touch, feel this character's energy moving through your hand. Recognize how this feels to you.

When you have fully acquainted yourself with the essence of this character, thank the character in your own way, and gently release your focus.

Then breathe deeply and return your attention to your body. Give yourself time to readjust your focus to your physical surroundings as you gently open your eyes.

Gift Exchange Meditation

In this meditation, you become quiet enough inside to feel an exchange of energy taking place between you and the dream character you have chosen to explore. It is a nice accompaniment to the Gifts adventure on page 63 in this chapter.

Adventure

> When you are ready to begin this adventure, take five slow, deep breaths . . . Feel each breath rise and fall . . . Slow yourself down inside as you do this. Let a feeling of warmth and peacefulness enter and fill you . . .
>
> Now focus on your dream character. Allow yourself to experience this character as a real "being," standing or sitting in front of you . . . Recognize how you respond to the presence of this being. Now imagine that there is energy — light, sound, or just a strong vibration — flowing from this character to you. Allow yourself to receive this energy. (If your dream character is at all frightening to you, imagine yourself in a protective encasement of light, where you can still feel and receive the energy offered you, but do not need to fear harm from it . . .) Also receive the knowledge that this character extends to you.
>
> Now, ask this character for a gift. Remember the first image that appears in your mind's eye when you ask, "What gift do you have to give me?" You will receive an image in your mind's eye that is a symbol of the gift this character has to give you. Allow this image to become clearer and clearer.
>
> Imagine your dream character surrounding this gift with golden light and offering it to you. In your own way, accept and acknowledge this gift.

Now feel energy flowing out from you to this character. Allow the character to receive your energy. Then recognize the knowledge that you have to give to this being. See this knowledge in symbolic form, as a gift that you can offer to this character. Watch for the first image that crosses your mind when you ask yourself, "What gift can I share with this being?" You will see a symbol of this gift in your mind's eye. Let this symbol become clear to you.

Surround this gift with golden light and present it to the character. Trust that your gift will be received in some way. Allow the character to acknowledge you and your gift.

Breathe deeply. In every relationship there is an exchange. Recognize the exchange taking place between the two of you . . . Realize the gifts you have shared. Take some time to experience this. When you feel you have absorbed the exchange, gently return your attention to your own body and breath.

Breathe deeply five times. As you do this, allow a feeling of warmth and peacefulness to fill you. Then when you feel ready, and not before, softly open your eyes. (If you would like to create symbols of these gifts you've exchanged, turn to the Gifts adventure on page 63.)

❧ *Movement* ❧

Basic Positions

One of the most ancient sources of wisdom available to us lies within our own bodies. And surprise, surprise — we can use the information that we receive from our bodies to give us insights into our dreams! I discovered this way of exploring dreams by examining my own dream image of a little frog twisting its way into my shoe. As I delved into this image, I found that this dream was encouraging me to start exploring my dreams in a more physical way. Before long I followed that suggestion and began creating some simple movement adventures, such as this one.

You'll be surprised at what you can discover when you crouch down on your hands and knees as one dream character, or teeter madly on your tiptoes as another. Just allow yourself to play with this adventure. And remember, if you need to clarify any of the experiences you have in this adventure, you can always engage in a writing, art, or meditation adventure afterwards.

Adventure

Find a position in which to put your body that feels like it symbolizes your dream character. You do not have to imitate the way the character actually looked in the dream. Instead, find a position that feels the way the spirit or energy of this character feels to you.

As you are discovering this position, you might want to consider the following questions. Does this character seem as though it needs to be low to the ground or up high? Is their energy heavy or light? Hard or soft? Active or passive? Consistent or wobbly? Strong or weak? Contracted or open?

Then, when you've settled into your body position, just pause and recognize what the position feels like. How does your body respond to this position? Is it a position that is familiar to your body?

Feel the energy of the character in your feet, calves, knees, thighs, abdomen, stomach, chest, buttocks, back, arms, hands, shoulders, neck, and face . . . Let yourself be filled with this character's energy. Now imagine that you are this character . . . Respond to the following questions as this character.

- Do you feel tension anywhere in your body?

- Is there some part of your body that feels like it is more vibrant than another part?

- Where do you feel the most weight in you?

- What is your deepest desire or goal?

- What knowledge do you have to offer?

- Do you feel whole or incomplete?

- What do you need to receive? What do you need to give?

Remaining in character, begin to explore some movements that seem as though they reflect your spirit, your deepest nature. You can add sounds if you like. Your sounds may include singing, spoken words, or other noises that you feel tell something about who you are.

After you've experimented with movement and sound for a bit, demonstrate what you were doing in the dream. Next, demonstrate what you were doing before you appeared in the dream. Then act out what you were doing after leaving the dream.

After you have finished these actions and you feel you have absorbed all the information you can by being this character, gently release this character's energy from your body. Then sit down, breathe deeply, and contemplate the part of you that this character represents.

Hand Movements

This is one of the simplest movement adventures you can embark upon. It helps you explore three different dream characters at once.

Preparation

Select three dream characters.

Adventure

Gently close your eyes. Relax . . . and picture the first dream character you have chosen. Contemplate this character and your response to this character's presence.

Now begin moving your hands in a way that reflects the nature of this character. Imagine that your hands are dancing and that their dance is silently telling the story of this character. Take as long as you need to experiment with these hand movements.

When you have done this, pause for a moment and consider this character as a part of yourself. Then relax, release this character from your focus, and go on to the second dream character you have chosen. Repeat this adventure with this character. Then go on and enter into this same adventure with your third dream character.

When you are finished exploring the third character, start making hand movements for the first character again. Go through the hand movements for all three characters without pausing. Every time you've finished with the movements for the third character, start your movements for the first character again, immediately. Continue through this cycle of movements until you can start to see a relationship between these three characters. (Do it at least three times without stopping.)

Now, let these movements begin to blend with one another. Let them transform each other. As the movements become blended, remember that each of these characters is a part of you. See what your hand movements are telling you about the ways these different parts of you want to grow and transform one another.

Body and Spirit

This adventure is a combination of two powerful adventures — Basic Positions and Verbal Dialoguing. I highly recommend it!

Preparation

Many of my students say that the easiest way to do this adventure is to record the following text on tape. If you leave long pauses between the instructions while you are reading, you can respond to them out loud when you are actually doing the adventure. However, if you do not want to tape it, you can either ask a friend to read the text to you slowly, or you can just keep your book open and near at hand as you enter the meditation, opening your eyes briefly for each new instruction.

Adventure

Close your eyes, relax, and breathe deeply . . . Find a position in which to put your body that feels the way the spirit or energy of your dream character feels to you. Now consider the following questions.

- Does this character's energy feel as though it is close to the ground, or up high?

- Does the energy of this character seem to be heavy or light? . . . Hard or soft? . . . Active or passive? . . . Consistent or wavering? . . . Strong or weak? . . . Contracted or open? . . . Old or new?

Now pause and recognize how this body position feels to you. How does your body respond to this position? Is this a position that's familiar to your body in any way?

Feel the energy of this character in your whole body, from your feet, up through your legs, torso, arms, neck, and head . . . Let yourself be filled with this character's energy.

Now imagine that you are this character . . . Answer the following questions out loud, as this character.

- How do you feel? Do you feel tension anywhere in your body?

- Is there some part of your body that feels like it is more vibrant than another part? . . . heavier than another part? . . . stronger than another part?

- Who are you?

- What do you have to tell the dreamer?

- Why do you try to reveal this information to them in the way that you did in the dream?

- What part of this dreamer do you represent?

- Can you suggest any new actions for the dreamer to take in their waking lives?

- What do you have to tell the dreamer about new ways to grow and love?

- Is there something else that you wish to share with the dreamer at this time, or do you feel as though this conversation is complete?

When this conversation is complete, begin to release the character's energy from your total focus. As you do so, remember that this character represents one part of you. You can learn from this part of you, nurture it, and encourage it to expand in new and different ways . . .

For now, just embrace this character as one aspect of your being as you return to a deeper awareness of your whole body and spirit . . . Then when you feel ready, gently open your eyes.

☙ *Eight-Day Dream Journey* ☙

The following guidelines can give you some assistance in deciding which dream adventures to participate in during an eight-day journey. Each day of this journey, you will need to choose one dream and a number of "characters" from that dream to explore (with the exception of Day 7, when you will examine one day in your waking life as though it were a dream). Characters are defined on page 28. The number of stars before each adventure indicates how many characters to explore with that particular adventure. For instance, in Day 2, I ask you to select a total of three characters. The single star (☆) in front of Free Association Writing indicates that you should explore one of those characters with Free Association Writing. The two stars (☆☆) in front of Rewording indicates that you should explore two of those characters through Rewording.

Suggested Adventures

Day 1

☆   Meditation with a Dream Character

☆   Free Association Writing

☆   Free Association Art

Day 2

☆   Free Association Writing

☆☆   Rewording

Day 3

☆☆   Point of View

Day 4

Themes
☆ Dialoguing

Day 5

☆ Dialoguing
☆ Gift Exchange Meditation and Gifts (use the same character)

Day 6

☆ Basic Positions
☆ Body and Spirit

Day 7

Record the events of a day in your waking life. Treat this "day" as though it were a "dream." Choose two characters from that day to explore, and then engage in the following adventures.

Themes
☆ Point of View
☆ Body and Spirit

Day 8

This is a full dream exploration involving three characters, so give yourself a little extra time this day to complete these adventures.

Themes
☆ Body and Spirit
☆ Gift Exchange Meditation
☆ Free Association Art
☆☆☆ Hand Movements (with all three characters you have just explored in the adventures listed above)

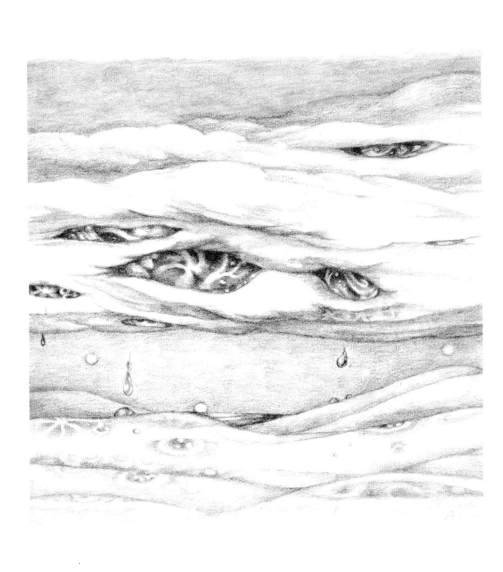

5

Waking Dream Adventures

You can embark on a dream journey by exploring a "waking dream" instead of a nighttime one whenever you wish. To begin this kind of a journey, first participate in an activity that allows you to expand your vision, such as dancing in an open meadow, gazing at the ocean, or engaging in one of the Waking Dream Adventures described in this chapter.

Once you have completed any of these activities, record the images that came to you during the experience and select several characters within them you would like to explore — just as you would with regular nighttime dreams. Then turn to one of the adventures described in the preceding chapter, and explore your waking dream characters using the guidelines described there.

Creating a Dream from Music

This is a soothing way to create a waking dream using one of your favorite pieces of music.

Preparation

Find a piece of music on a record or tape that you especially like. A piece without words would probably be best.

Adventure

Turn on the piece of music. Lie down or sit with eyes closed. Listen to the music and pay attention to what happens inside you as you do so.

Watch for images that pass by, hear any messages that come to you, and feel any feelings that move through you.

Don't force the dreams to come. When you see an image pass by, notice what you are seeing. If you hear a voice or phrase, just listen to it, and if you feel something, just breathe into this feeling and realize what that feeling is.

After the piece of music is over, open your eyes and anchor the dreams you just had by recording them in writing.

Starting with an Image

In this waking dream, you choose an image and create a dream that begins with that image.

Preparation

Pick an image from the list at the end of this adventure or make up one of your own.

Adventure

Lie down or sit with your eyes closed. Breathe deeply and relax.

Now focus on the image you have chosen. There is a dream that wants to unfold from this image. Let it begin to unfold now . . .

See, hear, and feel all the pictures, messages, and sensations that come to you for the next few minutes as you contemplate this image . . .

Let your attention flow from one impression to another, without trying to hold on to or suppressing any of them.

Other images will come to mind as you reflect on this image. Let them come. Notice your responses to these images too . . .

Then open your eyes and anchor your dreams by writing them down.

Suggested Images

a full moon

the first color that comes
to mind when you close
your eyes

the first animal that
comes to mind when you
close your eyes

something tiny,
then something huge

something hard, then
something soft

a fire or flame

a quiet place

a body of water

a road

a pair of shoes

the first plant that
comes to mind when you
close your eyes

an object, place, or
being that you knew in
your childhood

dawn and/or sunset

Starting with a Theme

In this waking dream, you generate a dream based on a theme.

Preparation

Select a theme from the list at the end of this adventure, or make up one of your own.

Adventure

Lie down or sit with your eyes closed. Focus on your theme . . . repeat it to yourself.

Now see, hear, and feel all the sounds, visions, and sensations that pass through your awareness as you focus on this theme . . .

Pay attention to your feelings about this theme . . . notice all your responses to it . . .

Then open your eyes and anchor your dreams.

Suggested Themes

Love	Travelling	Time	Adventure
Work	Happiness	Creation	Healing
Pleasure	Strength	Wisdom	Secrets
Challenges	Trust	Protection	Purpose

Waking Smell Dream

This simple adventure is initiated through one of your physical senses.

Preparation

Find some objects that have a fragrance. Pick some flowers . . . gather some seaweed . . . open a container of cinnamon . . .

Adventure

Close your eyes. Relax . . . Let any tensions you have been feeling be released with each breath . . .

Then breathe in the smell of your first object, and let the smell itself take you into a dream. Smell the object a number of times, and each time be aware of any feelings, messages, sounds, and images that pass through your consciousness. Take your time with this.

Then go on to your next object and repeat the process.

When you are finished smelling and dreaming about each object, open your eyes gently, and record your dreams.

Waking Touch Dream

This is another dream adventure that starts with physical responses to physical objects.

Preparation

Find several objects that have different textures — they could be hard, soft, prickly, fuzzy, slippery . . . one could be a leaf, one a wad of cotton, and one a rock.

Adventure

Close your eyes. Breathe deeply and allow yourself to become quiet inside . . .

Then pick up your first object. Feel it — touch it with your hands, lay it on different parts of your body — and as you do so, begin to dream. Allow feelings, sounds, messages, and images to pass through your awareness that arise out of your experience of this object. Breathe deeply and take your time with this. Then continue this same kind of discovery process with your next object.

When you have touched each of your objects and dreamed about them, open your eyes and start anchoring these dreams — noting them in some physical form.

Waking Taste Dream

This is another fun waking dream born in your physical body.

Preparation

Assemble several different kinds of foods, such as parsley, olives, crackers, peanut butter, milk, peaches, chocolate ice cream, or whatever else is in your kitchen.

Adventure

Close your eyes. Breathe and let your whole body relax . . .

Then pick up your first food. Taste it with your eyes closed. Be aware of the feelings, images, memories, or sounds that come to you as you do this.

When you have completed this experience with the first food, go on and repeat this process with the other foods.

Then open your eyes and record the dreams these tastes brought to you, either by writing, sketching, or combining the two.

Walking and Dreaming

This waking dream takes shape through movement and alertness.

Adventure

Take a walk. When you return home, write a description of some of the people, events, scenes, animals, plants, and thoughts that were a part of your walking adventure. Take particular note of those experiences that you least expected or that affected you the most.

Day Dream

Look at a day in your waking life as though it were a dream!

Preparation

Record the events of a day in your waking life. Be sure to include some of the details, although if your day was very busy you don't need to get too extensive with this.

Adventure

Look for themes in your day. (Themes are described on page 55.) Find relationships between your different experiences. Are there parallels or similarities between the events? Are there contrasts or differences? Did any of the events leave an especially strong impression on you? Were there any similarities or contrasts between the people, objects, and creatures you encountered?

After you have looked for themes and considered some of these questions, engage in some dream adventures with some of the characters in your day. (Remember, a "character" doesn't have to be a person. It could be a big dog, a copy machine, a black and stormy sky — any entity or object that had a strong impact on you.) I particularly recommend Dialoguing on page 49, Point of View on page 46, or Body and Spirit on page 72.

Male/Female Waking Dream

This adventure is both very fun and very revealing.

Adventure

Close your eyes. Breathe deeply and relax . . .

Now imagine yourself as a member of the opposite sex . . . how would you feel as a member of the opposite sex?

What would you look like? (Note: Your imagined "looks" as the opposite sex don't need to bear any relationship to your present looks, i.e., if you are a tiny, red-haired woman, you can still imagine yourself as a huge, black-haired man.)

Where would your home be?

What would you like to do the most?

What work would you do?

Would you be in an intimate relationship with someone?

What would your name be?

What would your friends be like?

What would your favorite adventures be?

Would you have any secret passions?

What else would your personality be like?

How would your personality be different than it is now?

After you have contemplated each of these questions, breathe deeply and gently open your eyes. Write down a description of yourself as a member of the opposite sex. Then you can try one of the Basic Adventures like Free Association Art on page 60, or Basic Positions on page 68 with this "character," if you like.

Meeting an Ancient Friend

This waking dream can take you into a deep, meditative state. I suggest that you ask another person to read this adventure to you, or that you record it on tape ahead of time, and play the tape back when you are ready to participate in it. This way you will have more freedom to relax and absorb the experience.

Preparation

Make sure that whoever reads these words does so in a quiet, peaceful voice, with good, long pauses between instructions.

As you listen to the instructions, share aloud the images that come to you. This will help you to stay focused more strongly on the meditation.

Adventure

Close your eyes. Breathe deeply . . .

Let each inhalation begin at your toes and travel upward, the full length of your body. Let each exhalation begin at the crown of your head and travel downward, all the way back to your toes . . .

Do five full breaths in this way.

Now just breathe fully and easily. Be aware of the way your breath cleanses your body . . .

Feel yourself extending in time and space with each breath you take . . . Give yourself room to *feel*. Let any obstacles to these feelings dissolve . . .

Be aware of your own spirit gently shining within your own body . . .

Grace the world with your willingness to be yourself now . . .

When you are willing to be yourself, you are like a glowing light. Imagine yourself as that glowing light now . . . like a star glowing in the world's great black, velvet sky . . .

Take some moments just to feel your light shining.

When you have done this, picture your light condensing into a star that comes and rests gently on your forehead.

This star illuminates a path that lies before you, a path that you need to see and feel and hear. It is the path of your secret dreams, your deepest yearnings and wishes . . .

Realize that this path lies before you, that you stand upon it . . . When you walk upon this path you will be moving in the direction of that which you love the most.

Walk upon this path now.

Notice all you can see . . .

Notice all you can hear . . .

Notice all you can feel . . .

Keep moving forward on this path. Eventually it will lead you to a special place where you can rest and your whole being can be refreshed, nurtured, and given the kind of care that you really need at this time . . .

This place can be a familiar place, or it can be one that is new in many ways . . . It is a place where you feel enveloped by love . . .

Once you have found this place, rest in it . . . Settle down . . . Be at ease . . . Allow any feelings of hurt or fatigue that reside in you to be gently touched and healed by the love in this place . . .

Take as much time as you need to with this . . .

Now let your gaze wander from the spot where you have planted yourself, and see as much of your surroundings as you can . . .

Listen to all you can hear here . . .

Recognize what this place feels like . . .

Be aware of the ways in which this environment reflects your own spirit . . .

Feel again how this place heals you . . . This is a home to which you can always return . . .

Linger in this place for a few moments more . . .

Now watch for the wise, old being who lives in this place, coming forward to greet you . . .

This being is a friend who can see all of you . . . who knows the path you have been walking on . . . who understands your deepest wishes and dreams . . .

Greet this old friend . . .

Now this being comes closer, gazes into your eyes for some moments, and then places a hand on your forehead . . .

As you experience this touch, you will begin to remember parts of yourself you have forgotten . . .

Let yourself see and appreciate yourself more fully now, and allow yourself to be loved by this being . . . Feel the love that emanates from your old friend as it enters your body and fills you . . . Feel it like a soft caress around your heart . . .

Surrender to this love and know that this love is safe. Your friend's tenderness, respect, and affection will always be with you . . .

As you receive this love, allow it to reawaken feelings of love, compassion, and humility within you . . . Let it teach you to recognize and accept your own unique, inner wisdom . . .

Bask in the experience of this love as long as you need to . . . Then return to your path with your old friend. This being knows your path.

Walk along together, and absorb all that you can see, and hear, and feel . . .

After you have walked a little way together, let this old being introduce you to a new place, a place for you to learn . . . Enter this place together.

Take your time to absorb your new surroundings. Use all of your awareness. See the environment as fully as you can . . . Listen to it . . . Feel it . . . Recognize the essence of this place . . . Now relax and spend as much time here, with your friend, as you need to . . . Then ask this wise being if he or she has anything else to share with you. Listen to the response. When you feel that the communication is complete, go ahead and share anything with your wise, old friend that you feel a desire to express.

Allow your friend to place a hand on your forehead again. Breathe deeply and remember all of who you are once more . . .

Again realize how much you are loved . . .

Then ask this wise being to bring his or her supportive presence into your heart . . . If your friend agrees, imagine this presence now entering your heart . . . Breathe deeply and feel what it feels like to have this being here . . .

Then ask this wise friend to light the lights in your heart every day . . . to help you to remember the deepest love that resides there . . .

Very gently, return your attention to your breath . . .

Ride each breath to its heights and travel down it to its deepest valleys . . . Breathe fully. Breathe in Life. Breathe in Love. Let your inner light shine as you renew yourself with your breath . . .

Feel light and love circulating within your own body . . . and feel light and love emanating from you as well . . .

Then become aware of physical reality around you . . . hear it and feel it . . . Recognize that this physical world exists simultaneously with your inner world . . . Prepare yourself to bring your inner glow back into the physical world . . .

Breathe deeply . . . Realize you are supported by the earth itself . . . Sink your roots down into it so that the light and love within you can grow and flourish . . . Be at home here on earth . . .

At the same time, recognize that your ancient friend, the one who sees you and remembers you, is returning to earth with you to give you strength and support . . .

Breathe deeply . . . Feel your breath coursing the length of your body . . .

Feel the way that your inhalation awakens new energy in your body . . . and the way that your exhalation releases distractions so that you can be more fully "present" at this time . . .

Reawaken into yourself . . . breathe . . . wiggle your fingers and toes. When you feel ready (and not before), gently open your eyes and readjust to your earthly home.

Now you can anchor this dream either by describing the images you saw in writing, or by sketching them.

Where Dreams Touch the Earth

The Dawning

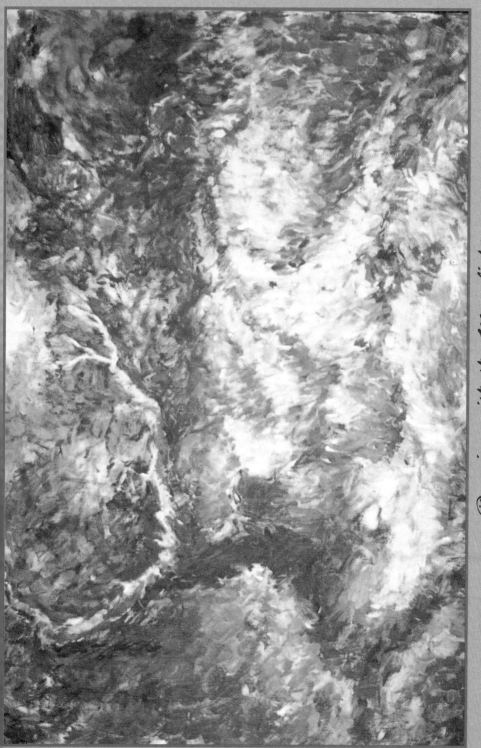

Dancing with the Moonlight

In the Depths

The Way Beyond

The Moon Goddess

*When the World Dreams of Wind
and Stars*

An Invitation to Dream

6

Advanced Dream Adventures

All the dream adventures in this book are like paths to your innermost self. The Basic Adventures in Chapter Four are the most direct paths; the Advanced Adventures in this chapter are more scenic and colorful routes. Both kinds of adventures are unique and valuable, yet I recommend that you explore the Basic Adventures before you move on to the ones in this chapter, if your intent is to reach a more in-depth understanding of your dreams.

Once you do feel ready to get acquainted with these adventures, read over them and just start experimenting. Then, if you would like more specific guidelines for a well-rounded dream exploration based on these adventures, turn to the Ten-Day Dream Journey described on page 150.

❧ *Advanced Writing Adventures* ❧

Informal Haiku

In most dream adventures, you attempt to bring some of the wisdom that is offered by a dream character into focus. At the same time, you don't want to define any part of your dreams too tightly. You want to maintain an appreciation of their fluidity, their various levels of meaning, and their magic. By writing haiku, you can explore the relationships between different aspects of your dreams without also making mincemeat out of them.

Adventure

Write a short, simple poem based on a character or characters from your dreams. You do not have to use any specific structure for this poem.

However, if you want to use a strict haiku structure, your poem should be three lines long and should have five syllables in the first line, seven in the second line, and five in the third line.

Dream Log 1

In one scene in this dream, I found that I could fly, but that I only skipped and glided low across the ground, because I was afraid to let go and leave the earth. In other scenes in the same dream, I encountered images and feelings that I associate with the ocean, each of which gave me a sense of openness and freedom.

> The ocean rolls free
> Not afraid to lose herself.
> I fly feet dangling.

Dream Log 2

I was part of a group of people that was watching a bunch of older couples. These older couples all knew each other and had decided to go square dancing. I thought they looked merry and strong. My group speculated about where they were going.

> The old men and women with arms linked
> Twirl the bright reds, yellows, and blues.
> When they stamp their feet
> They set the squares dancing.

Dream Log 3

A friend of mine came up to me and said she'd dreamed about milk and wood. I encouraged her to contemplate what milk and wood meant to her instead of seeing them as unchanging objects, separate from herself. In the following two haiku, I'm doing what I encouraged my friend to do in the dream — exploring what milk means to me in the first poem and what wood means to me in the second.

> Once arms cradled me
> I listened to the world's bells
> Calling, faraway.

> In woods, my grown heart
> Finds the places I've longed for
> My wildness comes home.

Dream 4

In this dream, I did not remember specific images, but I did retain a sense of vibrancy and expansion in my heart when I woke up. I felt that I had stepped into an experience of the underlying union of all beings — a union that I realized continues to exist even in the midst of my own distraction and struggling.

> The great circle sang
> Beyond the edge of my dream.
> My small heart listened.

Character Description

Ah, what joy comes from mingling your waking imagination with your dreams! This delightful adventure guides you through the process of developing a full, creative description of one of the characters in your dreams.

Adventure

Give yourself a few moments to contemplate the nature of your dream character . . . Recognize your own response to this character . . .

Now you are going to embellish the information that you received about this character through your dreams. Playfully imagine the circumstances of this character's life and "fill out the story" of this character's background.

The following questions can help you to do this. Read them over and then write to your heart's content, letting your imagination roam freely.

What does the character look like? What does he or she wear?

What does this character's voice sound like?

What has the most meaning to this character? What kind of purpose, goal, or work does this character have? What philosophy does he or she live by?

Where is this character's home and what does it look like?

What does this character most enjoy doing?

Who are this character's closest friends?

Has any change recently occurred in this character's life, or is there a change about to occur?

Remember that you don't have to answer all of these questions — they are just guidelines! Explore this adventure in your own way. Then consider the ways in which this dream character is a part of you.

Dream Log

I saw an unusual man in my dream who felt magical to me. He was dressed in orange clothes, containing a distinctive pattern. At one point we were in an empty room together, experimenting with some "natural law" like gravity. I had a very strong feeling of the absence of gravity and I think we were walking on the walls and ceiling or floating.

Character Description (Unusual Man)

He is a magical man, a wizard. I will call him Milel. Someone in another world created Milel by weaving him together out of sparkling threads of color. His clothes were woven together in the same way. They are predominantly orange, flecked with tiny bits of azure, crimson, green, and gold. Throughout these colors runs a distinctive pattern of dark lines. The pattern is a symbol of something, I think . . . it feels like a spell or the beginning of a story or an entryway to some mysterious experience . . . Yet it is a part of another language that I do not know.

Everything in the land Milel comes from, especially colors, shapes, and gestures, has a certain meaning, and this pattern does, too. When the people from that land speak, they use colors, shapes, and gestures to tell stories that touch each other deeply. Milel himself can gaze at a color and see the deep and subtle magic within it. And when he wishes to, he can look at a color and then travel through it, as if it were a tunnel to another world.

This special being comes to this world and finds much that he loves here. He is moved by the wind and the trees and draws endless delight from the animals. I would expect him to seem light and ethereal, but he is not at all. When he comes close to me he is deep and full. His nearness lures me down into a profound, rich valley within myself that I long for so often, but am afraid to go to. It is the place I have always yearned for, called "home."

With Milel near me, I *can* return home. There are no barriers between realities within him and he delights in that. He laughs at it and dances his dances from one realm to another. For him, it is the most natural thing in the world for me to be able to return home whenever I want and to be awake and alive. So I feel at home when I am with him.

Milel teaches me how to make "crossovers" in reality. In this dream he shows me how to walk through a world in which gravity does exist, while maintaining a state of consciousness in which there is no gravity.

Milel's whole life is an exploration of different realities and of ways of passing from one reality to another. Since he clearly understands that this is the task of his life, the essence of his experience does not shift much from one day to the next. However, his encounters with different beings do continually vary and surprise him, and *this* kind of change is a regular occurrence in his life.

Milel is the kind of friend who will always return to me through time, but who is not always visible to me in the way that I know how to see. He loves crossing over into other worlds and he goes to many others besides this one. He knows how to create new worlds, too, by weaving colors together or by moving his body in certain ways. Sometimes when I watch him creating, he seems to flicker before my eyes, like the fireflies I used to watch on late August nights as a child.

When Milel returns to his homeland, the place where the mirthful old woman once wove him out of many colors, he meets others who understand him and who can move through other realities with him. They can see him most of the time if they choose. So he does not yearn for a far-off home as I do. He knows that he is eternal, that he is always visible somewhere, and that whole worlds can arise out of his hands. Milel is happy in himself and he constantly moves and experiments with himself as if he were the colorful scarf appearing and disappearing in the magician's hand.

Waking/Dream Free Association

This adventure is a variation of Free Association Writing, found in Chapter Four. In this version of the adventure, you explore a character that appears both in your dreams and in your waking life.

Preparation

Select a dream character you have seen both in dreams and in waking life.

Adventure

Free-associate on the character as you know it in your waking life. Then free-associate on the character as you experienced it in your dreams. Remember to focus on what you feel each time.

Now compare the two free associations. What can you learn about this character from your two different experiences of it?

What does your dream version of the character show you that you didn't realize about the character in your waking life?

Dream Log

In this dream, I looked down from the top of the hill where I was standing, towards a group of buildings lining the banks of a canal. The scene reminded me of Venice. The buildings were in shadow and the sky around them was turning colors. Whether it was sunrise or sunset I was watching, I'm not sure.

Waking Life Free Association (On Venice)

Memories of Venice. Long, slender, delicate lines. Still water in tranquil canals. Arching bridges and people without cars, without boxes to hide in.

Venice is pure, exposed femininity. She is beautiful and graceful and ancient. All her streets, walls, and rooftops speak of art. Her churches are cluttered with paintings. The very air there seems thick with poetry . . . a poetry that is forgotten in many places nowadays . . . She is a remnant from days gone by when art rather than technology was the framework of people's lives. Once, years ago, she was a quiet, inspirational place for artists and writers to come and reflect on her silent water.

When I first met Venice in waking life, I was young. I had gone to Italy as an exchange student and was staying there with a wondrous family who had welcomed me in with open hearts. They took me to see Venice. Valla, the mother of this family, thought of Venice as her favorite city.

Dream Free Association (On Venice)

In this dream, Venice is bathed in darkness. A golden, reddish light shines behind the dark, curving shapes of her buildings. Is it sunrise, sunset? I am not sure. I just know it is a time of change, of transformation . . . and Venice is either arising in this moment and coming to life above the serene water . . . or she is dissolving at this time, making her peace and blending into the sunrise. It is a time of birth and death.

In either case, I feel my heart eased by this vision. Venice appears to me like a hope finally unfolded, an image of secret beauty revealed . . .

Discussion of Both Free Associations

When I saw Venice as a youngster, in waking life, I had less appreciation for her. I liked her, but she did not inspire the love that I felt for her in this dream. In this dream, however, I recognize Venice as an ageless vision, full of grace and elegance. She is a gentle spirit showing me her triumph in the changing light. She seems to be myself — my femaleness, my artistry, and my beauty. And she is like Valla, my sparkly-eyed "Italian mother," too.

The Venice of my dreams gives me hope in this time of change . . . She is arising or dissolving, or both. Either way, she is bringing me new life. Her subtle, artistic spirit is moving within me.

Theme Free Association

This is a nice addition to the Themes adventure on page 55. You can use it as a tool for delving into the messages offered by a whole dream (rather than a single character or scene).

Preparation

Select a whole dream; one containing a number of characters is best. Explore the themes or patterns within this dream (using the Themes adventure if you need assistance with this). Then begin this adventure.

Adventure

Write down the themes you have found and free-associate on one of them. You can do this in whatever way you choose. One way to free-associate on a theme is to pick one character from the dream and free-associate on it. Then examine the relationship between this character and the theme you are exploring. Ask yourself, "What does this character tell me about the theme?"

After you have done this, free-associate on other characters in the dream and describe their relationship to the theme also.

You don't have to write complete sentences. Let your writing flow. Explore the characters. Delve into the theme. And most importantly, remember to write down what you *feel*.

Dream Log 1

I was putting markers on a very high, steep hillside, far apart from one another. I heard a man telling someone else that the second marker I put in was almost impossible to reach. The next thing I knew, I was in a river that flowed down below these markers, looking at some other people who were downstream from me. They were being carried along by the river's current, right through some whitewater. I tried to position myself in the

*river so that the current would carry me to the place I wanted to go. Then
I let go and let the river carry me forward.*

*In another scene I was standing outside an aerobics class that I
had taken in the past, telling a friend that I and many others I knew no
longer came to this class because the physical exercises had just gotten
too difficult.*

*After that, I went into Phil's apartment to get some things. (Phil is
someone I know in waking life who, like myself, has created, packaged,
and marketed posters.) I didn't make any direct contact with him in the
dream — I just called to him as I left with the things I needed.*

Themes

Seeing I have a choice between two ways of doing things. The first
way involves increased effort and struggle on my part. The second
way involves being more receptive to help I can receive both from
my own "deeper flow of awareness" and from others around me.

Titles for this Dream

Tired of Steep Aerobics
Discovering my River Guide

Theme Free Association (Beginning with
Aerobics "Character")

I get tired of too many jumping jacks and I get tired of searching
for too many unknown answers. There seem to be so many pieces
involved in making a dream or a creation into a solid thing sometimes. I lose my passion in trying to compile all the pieces,
remember all the details, and do the aerobics of expressing myself
in the world.

I have forgotten the river. I have forgotten that more activity
and more goals require more dreaming. I have forgotten that this
man Phil who has created his own posters might have the information that I need to be able to package my posters . . . that the
dream state might be able to give me this kind of information
that I need to proceed in my waking life. I have forgotten that
opportunities could come to me, or that I could be gentle with
myself and flow forward, gathering the fulfillment of my needs
along the way.

In this dream, the goals set upon the hillside are too far away and too tremendous to reach. But the goals downstream, in the flow of the river, are more accessible. This suggests to me that when I can find the "current" in myself — the area of focus where my love and passion presently feel the strongest — then my life will flow more easily. The river of energy flowing through my being will give me the answers I need. I must trust in myself and in that river.

Dream 2

In one scene from this dream, I was preparing to ride down a hillside on a pony. I intended to retrieve something that my mother and father valued, but had left behind. I was starting the journey at night and realized I might have to make two trips to retrieve whatever it was I was seeking.

Then I was approaching a university. I discovered that those who wished to enter this university had to demonstrate their ability in cheerleading. "Uh oh," I thought. "I'm probably going to feel pretty uncoordinated and silly doing that."

The next thing I knew I was standing in front of some shelves at the university, trying on some sweaters. One was a soft, fuzzy, yellow cardigan. While I was looking at the sweaters, I was conscious of the fact that a man I felt really close to was at the bottom of a nearby hill, about to try and ride up the hill on his bicycle. For a flash of a second, I felt great despair. I realized that 95% of his experience so far indicated that he had no chance to make it . . . and I didn't think he would either.

In the next instant, I realized he would make it up the hill, precisely because the odds against him were very great. To face this challenge, he would bring his will to bear in the bike ride and he would make it.

In the next scene in this dream I walked around to the other side of the shelves where I had been looking at sweaters. There were lots of books on the shelves on this side. A man standing not too far away from me said he hadn't found any good books here or anywhere — books that shared some sort of deep, beautiful vision of the author's. He didn't think any had been published.

I knew differently. I went over to him and began showing him a number of the books. One of these was a story about a man who loved a tree . . . (or a man who loved an animal — I'm not sure which). Next to it was the sequel to this story. There were many other wonderful books by a number of different authors all around these.

When I woke in the morning following these dreams, I felt a great sense of hopefulness stirring within me.

Themes

That which is good is being brought forth and acknowledged . . . it is succeeding. This is a dream of hope.

Titles

Cheerleading for Dreams
Hope Rising Up Hills and Through Books

Theme Free Association (Beginning with my Journey Downhill)

Down at the bottom . . . something almost forgotten, but not forgotten by love . . . something cherished by my father and my mother, but left behind because they did not think they could bring it with them. I see it as a thing of value and I go back to get it. I want to retrieve it because I love them. And there is joy in that journey and a sense of the heroic . . . not because I saved something of theirs, but because my journey shows that that which is most secretly, deeply loved and most valuable to a human being is always retrievable. This is a time for the saving of things. These dreams are full of promise . . . of acknowledging that which is good and right and worth celebrating. A friend who is faced with great odds rides against these odds and conquers them; new, strong books line the shelves, and I am asked to try cheering. I am seeing all of life in this dream wrapped in a warm sweater of hope.

What I am learning to see more clearly in this dream is the others striding up the hills with me. My books of delicate, magical woods and hidden dreams revealed are not the only sparkling books on the shelf. Others are speaking, too. And just as I was able to ride in the first dream and save a dream of my mother's and father's, so there will be others to ride for *me*. In days to come, there will be many riders taking their ponies down the slopes. And many of these will bring new hope back with them.

Scene Description

In this adventure, you examine a scene from your dreams, letting it blossom in your awareness. By calling on your memory of the scene as you saw it in the dream, your emotional response to that scene, and your imagination, you develop a full description of that scene in writing.

Scene description, like character description, offers you a wonderful beginning for a creative writing project. It is also helpful at those times when you wish to unfold the meaning of a dream, but a more direct route, like engaging in Themes or Dialoguing, does not seem to work for you.

Preparation

Choose a dream *scene,* rather than a character, to explore. (Scenes are defined on page 29.) Make sure your scene is one in which the setting for the events taking place is at least partially clear to you.

Adventure

Focus on the scene at hand and write down some details of it. Some of these details you will remember directly from the dream itself. Others you will not remember and will need to create now from your imagination.

For instance, if you don't remember hearing anything in the scene, imagine what you could have heard. If you don't remember looking at the sky in your dream, reenter the dream now in your imagination, look up at the sky, and see what it looks like.

Let this dream scene come alive. Some of the following questions can assist you in this process.

- What is the tone or mood of this scene?

- What are the main colors within this scene? What kind of light is there within this scene?

- How do the light and shapes within this scene feel to you?

- What sounds can you hear here?

- What smells can you smell here?

- Are there people, creatures, objects, and plants within the scene? What are they like?

- Is there any activity happening within this scene?

- What events are taking place here?

- What can you see in each direction?

- What is below your feet and above your head? What is around the corner or over the horizon?

- Are there any events that seem to have just happened here? Are there any events that seem about to happen here?

Now contemplate the whole scene as if it were one presence. Notice how the different aspects of the scene — the feel of the trees, the smell of the earth, the calling of the birds — are all like reflections of one living presence.

Feel your own responses to this scene and its "presence." Include this in your written description, if you haven't already.

Dream Log

I am travelling on the road through Moonstone Heights, wearing a red raincoat. Off to the left people are fighting in the woods. It is pouring rain.

Scene Description

Everywhere there is this rain, this wetness, this heaviness of water carried in one's pockets and shoes. I feel as though it has been raining forever. As I go up the road to Moonstone Heights, I see people chasing each other in the wetness. The blue-grey road I travel on is open and smooth — but their people are not on that road. They are struggling amidst the forest of bare winter trees, splashing in the mud, fighting with branches.

Sometimes it looks as though these people are breaking the branches of quiet trees or hitting at anyone who comes close enough for them to hit. Yet I know that this is an illusion. Actually, these people are fighting with their own demons. They are afraid to admit their own feelings and are fighting with their own sorrow. Instead of admitting the unhappiness within themselves, they tell themselves that the trees are poking at them, and they lash out.

In contrast to them, I am feeling warm, dry, and contemplative inside my red raincoat. Today I am not involved in the fray. Today I just watch and understand.

As I move closer to these people, my quietness meets the woods' quietness and merges with it. I remember that the trees know me. Once again, I appreciate my own warmth and dryness. I realize that I and those close to me have cared enough about me to see that I am well clothed. The raincoat and boots are a sign to me of my own ability to preserve who I am.

I leave this field of people as quietly as I came and go on up the road. I do not want to change the weather. I like the pensive, shifting sky and the moist smell of the earth. I do, however, look forward to a warm fire and a hot drink I know I can find at home.

Expanded Self Writing

In this nurturing and rejuvenating adventure, you explore an image of what you would be like if you allowed yourself to reside at the center of your own inner wisdom. This vision of yourself accepting your own wisdom is what I call your "expanded self." It is your true self. It is a picture of what you would be like if you let yourself be who you really are — if you let yourself express your real beauty and strength.

Now most of us need some tools to help us talk to our true selves. This adventure can provide you with those tools. By following the guidelines given here, you will meet your expanded self as a living presence, full of color, texture, and vibration. You will see that your expanded self lives in you and that it is an ancient part of yourself that is more than willing to communicate with you. You will also get to see how your expanded self can transform both dream and waking life events. In other words, you will learn how you would respond to any given situation if you were approaching it from the center of your own power and wisdom.

Preparation

Either look for an expanded self character in your dreams, close your eyes and imagine a specific image of your expanded self as you see it at this moment, or take a walk in the physical world and ask "the universe" to show you an image of your expanded self.

Expanded self characters include images that:

- seem awesome to you in some way;

- give you a particularly good feeling, a sense that miracles might be possible, or a sense of something magical vibrating on the edge of your awareness;

- let you see yourself crossing the bounds of what you consider to be the limits of physical reality — undergoing physical transformation yourself, flying, being able to breathe underwater, etc.;

- have a great intensity of some sort — such as particularly strong colors, large size, great beauty, power, depth, great joy or merriment, a strong feeling of freedom or unlimited potential, or deep wisdom and understanding;

- contain a wide spectrum of life forms within them;

- are emitting a great deal of light or an extremely strong vibration.

After you have identified an expanded self character, choose a situation that you have experienced either in your dreams or your waking life that you would like to explore. (One in which you experienced feelings of conflict might be best.)

Adventure

The first step in this adventure is to enter into some Dialoguing with your expanded self character. Dialoguing is described on page 49.

The next step is to describe the dream situation or waking life situation you've chosen as fully as you can on paper.

After you have done this, rewrite that situation by describing what happens when you bring your expanded self into this situation with you.

Notice how the presence and support of your expanded self changes your own responses.

Notice how the presence of your expanded self transforms other aspects of the situation as well.

If you feel that this character would take any action to change the situation, realize what this action and its effect would be. Record all your impressions.

Waking Dream Log

One day in my waking life, I found an expanded self character when I was feeling depressed and had taken a walk down to the beach. As I walked along I saw some huge old cypress trees on a ridge, overlooking the dunes. I felt an impulse to go and stand under them. When I did so, I felt warmed and reassured. I realized that these beings were symbols of my expanded self and that they had some wisdom to pass on to me. When I returned home, I sat down and wrote out the following dialogue with one of with the trees.

Me: Tree, what do you have to tell me?

Tree: The earth is rich, it is deep, all kinds of life forms come out of it. You have your own fertile soil within you that is like the earth. Many dreams are ready to grow outward from it. Trust in this. Incubate the dreams that you would like to see growing in the physical world at this time. Feed them from the earth itself. Grow in places where you are fed by images of manifestation. Go to bookstores to feed your writing. Go to art galleries to feed your art. Meet others who are manifesting. Trust yourself. The struggles come only when you forget what you already know. Nourish yourself, feed yourself with the joys of the earth, and practice *remembering*. The trees and the earth will help to remind you of the truths that you know.

Me: What part of me are you?

Tree: I am the channel through which your spirit connects with the earth. You have me within you but you forget this, because you must move in your life and you get distracted thinking about all the choices of movement that are available to you. If you wish to remember the "me" that is in you, you might try visualizing your-self as the "dancing tree." That way your receptive channel can be open, and yet you can still feel strong and solid and able to move in the physical world.

First Dream

I approach my father, knowing he has cancer. He looks tired and unwell, but he says he'd be willing to try some healing through visual-ization. I am overjoyed, feeling that this time, there is a strong possi-bility that he will live.

(In contrast to this dream, my father did not experiment with any alternative healing methods while he was alive. He did die of cancer a number of years ago.)

First Rewrite with the Expanded Self, the Tree

My father is fragile. And the wrinkles in his skin, his tiredness, and the sickness in his body have all added a little heaviness that he has had to carry around.

Yet now he has made a courageous decision. Weak and tired as he is, he had decided to choose life. This time, if hope is offered to him, he will take it. Once he was not able to rise up in this way. Now I see him making a new choice.

I am overjoyed. My father is a dear, sweet man and I love him deeply. With all my heart, I have always wished that he could know newness and magic in the foundations of his life . . . that his joy could be more than a brief melody, a few poetic words.

He is like the little elf in each of us now . . . no great, shining knight, but a small, stubborn, hobbit-like spirit that rises up in the midst of despair and says, "I cannot see the stars. I have not heard laughter for a long time. But I trust they are there, and I will go on."

And I know that my father lives in me somewhere, too. This dream does not just indicate change for my father in that other dimension where he now exists . . . it also indicates that I am making a shift at the base of my own life. I too am opening up, preparing for a new journey, hoping to recover some starlight.

Yet love feels stiff in me sometimes. It is deep and I feel it at my roots, but I don't know what to do with it. When my father tells me he is now open to visualization work, I blink at him dumbly. It is my old tree self that goes to him first and lays its branches gently across his chest and around his body. The tree knows that he is tired, spent . . . that he has used all the strength he could conceive of in asking for new direction in his life . . . and that he needs contact with trees and other earthly beings most of all, at this time.

My father closes his eyes now and nestles down in the tree branches. The tree hums in a low voice, soothing him so that he can sleep.

It is time for me just to watch and learn from my tree at this point. I have always thought I was supposed to heal my father with new ideas and techniques. I didn't realize that what my father needed most at this time was to be loved, touched, and reassured . . . to receive acknowledgment for the courage he has shown thus far.

Gradually, however, I realize that it is time for my father to rest now and start to come to peace with himself before he goes on in new directions. When I finally grasp this, I too go to my father and gently lay my hands on him.

Second Dream

I am staying with a male friend in a room that feels somewhat sleazy. Someone is knocking at the door. I think it is a woman. My friend answers the door, but soon closes it again. When I ask him who is there, he says he doesn't know. I go over to the door and push the button lock on the doorknob. Yet, I still don't feel safe enough. So I ask the man to switch sides before we get into bed so that he will be closer to the door and I will feel more protected.

I realize, uneasily, that there are holes in the walls and that people outside can look in, if they want to.

Second Rewrite with the Expanded Self

In the middle of this sleazy place, the tree suddenly appears. It came when I asked it to come. Now it stands warm, attentive, and fully visible, waiting to see how it can help.

The tree does not doubt its own strength. It is solid and full of humor. If it had eyes, they'd probably be sparkling. I feel more secure just being near the tree in this scene. Its steadiness helps me to relax.

The tree is also not afraid of other beings who try and make contact with it. In its own warm, humorous, and yet powerful way, it is always ready to meet any beings who seek it out. Because of this, it is unshaken by those who peer in through the holes in the wall. It knows that these beings are just curious, and helps me to see that they are not harmful.

And it is not afraid of the knocking, either. When the knocking comes, the tree faces the door. Having this tree next to me, I sense my own strong roots in the earth, and I too am willing to face the door. In this way, the tree helps me to make contact with a new being.

This being turns out to be a woman. When she sees the tree (my expanded self), she gives it a big hug. They seem to know each other well. The tree knows her purpose in life and they talk about it. She tells the tree that she has been out walking in the rain, along Elm Street, where I used to walk to school as a child. I remember that I used to be afraid of the street, because of a big row of dead trees that lined the sidewalk there. This strong young woman does not speak of the street with fear, however. She just says that she was glad to leave there so that she could come in out of the rain.

After a moment, the tree introduces me to her. It tells me that she is my future self. I can hardly believe it. She strikes me as someone who is much stronger than I am now. I still struggle with a lot of fear in my life. She, on the other hand, no longer focuses on her fears, but moves through the world empowered by a strong awareness of her own intent.

She, too, is incredulous that I am a part of her and scrutinizes me closely. Then, before little time has passed, she stops, laughs in merriment, and thanks the tree for introducing us.

Our communion touches me. I am not sure we would have seen or acknowledged each other as part of one another if the tree had not been there. Yet the tree, who is a symbol for love, the timeless awareness within both of us, knows that we are one and allows us to meet through its presence.

❧ *Advanced Art Adventures* ❧

Art in Combination with Haiku

Often a combination of art and writing adventures can enhance one another. Try this "combination adventure" and see what you think.

Preparation

Read the Informal Haiku adventure on page 96. Then collect some paper (I suggest that you use construction paper or some finer quality paper sold in an art store, rather than newsprint).

Adventure

Write a simple poem about your dream character, following the suggestions in the Informal Haiku adventure. Copy this poem either onto one side of the paper, or into the middle, with space around it, like so:

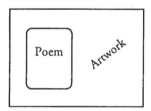 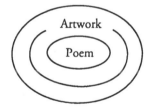

Now imagine the poem in visual form. How could you express the feeling of the images using colors, textures, shapes, or drawn symbols?

Create pictures or patterns representing this poem around the written words, using materials from your art box.

When you are done you will have two complementary reflections of your dream: one in haiku and one in art.

Companion Adventures

From Chapter 6, *Advanced Writing Adventures:* Informal Haiku.

Collage

With this kind of collage, take a big piece of paper and place on it the mixture of magazine pictures, colors, shapes, and textures that you feel reflects a theme from one of your dreams.

Preparation

Collect a newsprint roll from your local newspaper office or go to an art store and buy a large newsprint pad. Gather a pile of magazines, some scissors, and glue.

Now select a dream and find the central themes within it, using Themes on page 55. Write down several words that describe one of these themes.

Adventure

Cut a large piece of newsprint into the shape you'd like your collage to be. We usually work on big rectangles in my classes, but other shapes like circles, ovals, triangles, or amorphous blobs are fun, too. Just remember to keep the shape you cut out *big*. It will fill up faster than you expect.

Now focus on the theme you have chosen to explore. Leaf through your magazines and cut out any pictures that you think are related to this theme. For instance, if the theme you were exploring was "power," you might look through the magazine and cut out pictures that you thought showed either great power or a lack of power.

Make a pile of these pictures. When you think you have plenty of pictures, glue them onto the paper. You can either lay them right next to each other, overlap them, or leave gaps between them. Gaps between pictures can be filled in with colors, drawn designs, and other materials from your art box, like glitter, lace, or foil, that seem like they fit the themes you are exploring.

When you have finished your collage, consider what it has to show you about the theme it reflects and the dream within which you found that theme.

Companion Adventures

From Chapter 4, *Writing:* Themes.
From Chapter 6, *Advanced Writing Adventures:* Theme Free Association.

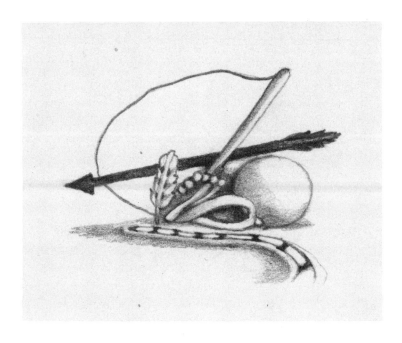

Dream Pillowcases

When you create art based on your dreams and then place it in a prominent place in your home, its presence starts to have an effect on you. In a subtle way, you allow your waking life to grow a little more integrated with your dream life. This particular adventure helps you to translate a scene from your dreams into something very tangible that you will see and touch almost every day — your pillowcase.

Preparation

You'll need a pillowcase (washed and ironed) and a box of fabric crayons, which are sold at almost all craft stores. Then select one scene from a dream that you'd like to explore.

Adventure

Remember this scene as clearly as you can and then depict it on your pillowcase. There are two ways you can do this. One way is to focus on the mood of the scene, how it feels to you. Then create colors and shapes on your pillowcase that you think reflect this mood.

The other way to enter into this adventure is to draw the actual scene as you remember it from your dreams. You might want to make a little sketch with crayons on another piece of paper first. Then go ahead and draw this scene on your pillowcase, using the fabric crayons.

When your pillowcase is finished, follow the instructions in the fabric crayon box that tell you how to preserve your artwork. You will either need to place a piece of paper over your drawing and iron it, or turn the pillowcase inside out and iron the back side of the design. Then wash your pillowcase. (The design will probably fade a little.)

Companion Adventures

From Chapter 6, *Advanced Writing Adventures:* Scene Description.

Dream Character's Home

In this adventure you explore the essence of a dream character by depicting the environment in which you think this character would feel the most comfortable.

Preparation

Gather a shoebox or some other container of similar size.

Adventure

Quietly close your eyes and contemplate your dream character . . . Imagine the kind of environment in which this character lives. Is it a pine forest, a large, noisy city, or near the banks of a rushing river?

Envision your character in their native surroundings. Then imagine the specific place within these surroundings that your character would call home. Is it a log cabin, a hollow tree stump, or on top of a cloud?

Is this home outdoors or indoors? How big is it? Are there neighbors nearby? Is this home light or dark? What does it smell like? Are there decorations in it? What are the predominant colors? Are there clothes, foods, pieces of furniture, musical instruments, or tools in it?

After you have imagined all you can about this character's home, open your eyes. Then create a representation of this character's home in your shoebox, using materials from your art box.

Companion Adventures

From Chapter 4, *Meditation:* Meditation with a Dream Character.
From Chapter 6, *Advanced Writing Adventures:* Character Description.

Scene in a Shoebox

With this adventure, you can see, touch, and explore a scene from your dreams. In this way, the scene itself blossoms more fully in your awareness.

Preparation

Find a shoebox or a container of similar size (no smaller than a shoebox). Then choose a dream scene to explore.

Adventure

Breathe deeply. Close your eyes and begin to absorb this scene. Remember all the details you can. If parts of the scene are hazy in your memory, imagine what they might have been like. Fill in gaps with your imagination.

Was this scene light or dark or somewhere in between? Was it inside or outside or partially enclosed? What colors, sounds, textures, and smells were a part of this scene? Did you see plants, animals, people, objects, or buildings in the scene?

If this scene took place outside, was there water nearby? What did the sky look like? What could you see in the distance?

What was the mood of this scene?

When you think you have a pretty clear image of this scene in your mind, open your eyes. Then create this scene in your shoebox, using the materials in your art box.

Companion Adventures

From Chapter 6, *Advanced Writing Adventures:* Scene Description; *Advanced Meditation Adventures:* Scene Meditation.

Mandala and Mobile

The following mandala and mobile adventures are really the same adventure — one is just two-dimensional and the other is three-dimensional. Both of them help you to explore the relationship between two different dream characters.

Mandala Preparation

Get a large piece of paper. Decide on two characters from the same dream to explore.

Mandala Adventure

Draw three big, concentric circles on your piece of paper. Each of the outer rings will represent one of the two dream characters you have chosen. You will use the area inside the innermost circle too, however, so make sure you keep it large enough so that you will be able to create some artwork within it.

Now close your eyes and focus on one of the characters. Feel the affect this character's presence has on you. Then imagine yourself exploring this character fully. Use your intuition and your physical senses to discover information. Watch, listen, touch — even smell — this character.

If this character has eyes, look into them. If the character is a tree or something else that you don't think has eyes, imagine that this character has eyes and then gaze into them.

Learn about the spirit of this character. Recognize the particular form of wisdom this character has to offer. Realize why this character has come to share this wisdom with you.

Then breathe deeply and open your eyes. Find the colors, shapes, textures, and drawing materials in your art box that you think reflect this character, and place these in the outermost ring of the mandala.

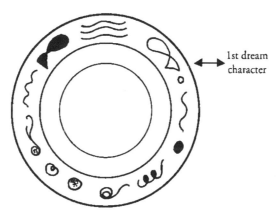

1st dream character

Then go on to your second dream character and repeat the same process I just described. This time, however, put the art materials reflective of this character in the ring that is adjacent to the one you just filled. When you are done with this, you should have one empty, circular area left in the middle of your mandala.

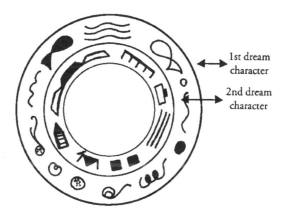

1st dream character

2nd dream character

Now close your eyes and picture both of the characters you just worked with in your mind's eye. Imagine these two characters overlapping. See them mingling, interweaving, and dancing with each other. What are the threads that tie these two characters together? What do they have to learn from one another? How can they strengthen each other?

Imagine them working together to support one another . . . At the same time, imagine them transforming each other . . . Allow their two images to begin merging together, in your mind's eye. Let them become one blended image . . .

When you have done this, open your eyes and begin to put colors, shapes, textures, patterns, and symbols in the innermost circle of your mandala that you think represent the integration of these two characters. Contemplate these two characters as parts of yourself that are seeking to become more interwoven.

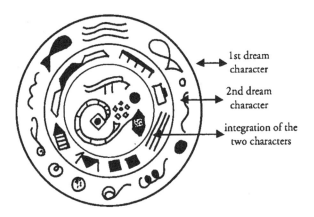

Note: If the integration of these two characters isn't completely clear to you and you don't know what image to create in the center of your mandala, look at the colors, textures, shapes, and symbols you have placed in the two outer rings of the mandala. Now bring some of the visual elements inside these two rings together into a unified design in the center. For instance, if there were jagged lines inside one ring, and smooth, curving shapes in the other, you would create a design in the center of the mandala that blended the jagged lines and the curving shapes.

When you have finished the center design, reflect quietly on your whole mandala. See if it has anything else to teach you.

Then turn to the Dialoguing adventure in the Writing section and enter into a dialogue with one or both of your dream characters. Make sure to ask these characters about their relationship to one another during the dialogue. This will help you to see these characters as parts of yourself that can work together for your own growth.

Mobile Preparation

Choose two characters from the same dream, just as in the adventure described above. Gather the materials you will need to create the structure of a mobile. Some of these materials might include string, thread, yarn, sticks, a hanger, paper, an embroidery hoop, or an old lampshade.

Mobile Adventure

This is another version of the mandala adventure, as I mentioned before. The only difference between this version of the adventure and the mandala version is that a mobile is three-dimensional and it moves!

To enter into this adventure, follow the same basic guidelines that I offered you for the mandala adventure.

Create a design that represents your first character and hang this on one of the outer edges of your mobile. Create a design that represents your second character and place this on another outer edge of your mobile. Then contemplate what the integration of these two characters would look like. Place a design that represents this integration in the center of your mobile.

Take a look at the following diagrams to give you some ideas of ways this mobile could be put together. Then go ahead and create!

If the structure of your mobile is something as simple as a stick or hanger, you might have a mobile that looks like one of these two pictures:

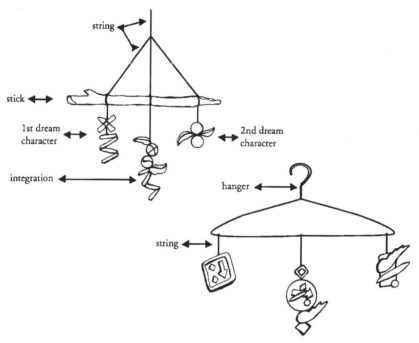

A paper and string mobile might look something like this:

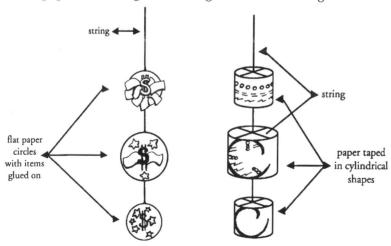

Lastly, if you use an old lampshade or an embroidery hoop with two strings crossed in the middle, you might put together a mobile that looks something like this:

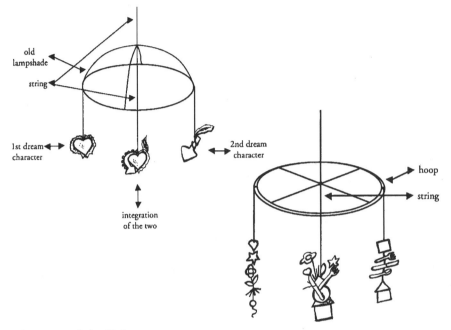

Companion Adventures

From Chapter 4, *Writing:* Dialoguing; *Meditation:* Meditation with a Dream Character; *Movement:* Any of these adventures.

Dream Circles

In this adventure, you create symbols for events that happened in the same dream and look for patterns between them.

Preparation

Decide on a whole dream you would like to explore. Then find a large sheet of paper.

Adventure

Create symbols for as many events in the dream as you can, placing these inside circles on your sheet of paper. Then examine each of the symbols separately, jotting down notes on them if you wish. Consider the ways in which each of these symbols is a part of you.

Now look for relationships between these different symbols. What is similar about them? What is different about them? Can you examine these symbols collectively and uncover some of the themes within this dream? Can you make up some titles for this dream?

Contemplate the symbols and the threads you see between them, and glean as much as you can from this dream.

Companion Adventures

From Chapter 4, *Writing:* Themes.
From Chapter 6, *Advanced Writing Adventures:* Theme Free Association.

Masks

By making a mask that represents one of your dream characters, you create a symbol that mirrors that character's spirit. If you like, you can use this mask in one of the Group Movement adventures in Chapter Seven (Dream Dance, Acting Out a Dream, or Dressing up as a Dream Character).

Preparation

First you need to collect a "base" or "foundation" for your mask. This base can be a paper bag, a paper plate, or one of those over-the-eyes, plain, black, Lone Ranger masks you can buy at a dime store.

If you are going to use the dime store mask and would like to fashion papier-mâché features onto it, you should place a few preliminary layers of papier-mâché on it now, before beginning this adventure. (Tear some strips of paper, dip them into a mixture of flour and water, and then layer them on.) Don't worry about shaping the papier-mâché into features yet — you will do that later.

The other kind of base you could use for your mask would be formed with a box of Plaster of Paris casting material that is sold in rolls at crafts stores and medical supply stores. For this kind of base, you will also need to have a little Vaseline on hand.

For each type of masks you will need some paint, a brush, and elastic or yarn to tie it on. Bring out your art box, too, so that you can glue other materials to your mask, like glitter and feathers.

Adventure

Relax. Close your eyes. Take a slow, full breath and imagine your dream character in front of you. Feel the spirit of this character. Observe all that you can. Now imagine that you are exploring each other. Watch one another, listen, touch, smell, and converse. Gaze into one another's eyes. (If this character is one like a tree, that doesn't have eyes, imagine what these eyes might look like, and then gaze into them.) Do whatever you need to do to get to know this character. Then open your eyes.

Create a mask that represents the character's spirit. The mask doesn't have to look like the character, it just has to reflect the spirit of the character.

Here are some different ways you could proceed, depending on the type of base you have chosen to use for the mask.

Paper Plate or Paper Bag Mask

Hold the plate up to your face, or put the paper bag over your head. Feel with your fingers where your eyes and mouth are and mark these with a magic marker. Next, take off the plate or paper bag and cut eye holes and a mouth hole in your mask. Then glue different materials onto your mask, adding paint if you like.

Dime Store Mask

Glue things onto this mask or add more papier-mâché to it, making features or shapes, if you've already applied some papier-mâché. Apply paint once it has dried.

Plaster of Paris Casting Material Mask

Gather your box of casting material, scissors, a large bowl of water, a jar of Vaseline, a towel, and a friend or two who will layer the Plaster of Paris on for you.

First of all, cut part of the Plaster of Paris roll into strips of various small shapes and sizes. You are going to need enough strips to make a mask several layers thick, so make sure you have a big pile of strips cut before you begin. Now, decide whether you want to create a half-mask, or a full-face mask. Put Vaseline on any parts of your face where the mask is going to touch. Make sure you grease right up to your hairline.

You are now ready to begin the mask making. Lie on your back and have your friend dip a Plaster of Paris strip in the water, wring it our slightly, and place it on your face. He or she will proceed in this way, covering all of the Vaselined part of your face with a layer of overlapping strips. When the first layer is complete, a second, and possibly a third can be added.

Inevitably, the water on the strips will run down your face and into your ears, so make sure your friend has a towel handy to wipe you off regularly. While this is happening, remember not to laugh! If you talk or laugh too much, you will jiggle the mask and bend it or tear it before it dries. For this reason, this form of mask making is really a meditation in itself.

You'll know when the mask is dry because it will no longer feel cold and clammy. It will have a funny, warm feeling instead! This should take about five to ten minutes. If you want to speed up the process, your friend can blow warm air on your mask with a hair dryer.

When you think the mask is dry, peel it off gently. Set it aside for a few minutes to make sure that it is completely dry.

When it is dry, you can add more papier-mâché or Plaster of Paris strips if you wish to alter the shape of the face. You might want to put bigger, more prominent features on it if the character the mask represents is a person, or a horn or beak on it if the character is some kind of animal.

Then, after the mask has dried this second time, you can go ahead and paint your mask with acrylic or latex paint and glue other materials onto it.

Companion Adventures

From Chapter 4, *Writing:* Dialoguing, Point of View; *Meditation:* Meditation with a Dream Character; *Movement:* Body and Spirit.
From Chapter 6, *Advanced Writing Adventures:* Character Description.

❧ *Advanced Meditation Adventures* ❧

Meditation on a Theme

This adventure helps you to examine one of the themes you have found in your dreams so that you can absorb it more deeply.

Preparation

Find a theme using the Themes adventure on page 55.

Adventure

Gently close your eyes. Breathe fully and relax as you focus on your theme. Contemplate what this theme is all about. What part of your own inner wisdom does it help you to remember? Quietly say to yourself, "This theme helps me to remember that _____," and fill in the blank.

Breathe deeply. What does this theme tell you about the choices you are making in your life? Quietly say to yourself, "This theme reminds me that I can choose _____ or I can choose _____," and fill in the blanks.

Breathe deeply. What does this theme have to tell you about ways you can experience love more deeply? Quietly say to yourself, "This theme suggests that I can experience love more deeply by _____," and fill in the blank.

Reflect gently on these messages. Also, remember to watch for more information about this theme as you return your attention to your waking life.

Then breathe deeply. Become more aware of your own body and environment. When you feel ready, and not before, gradually open your eyes. Take the transition time you need . . . and return your focus fully to the physical world.

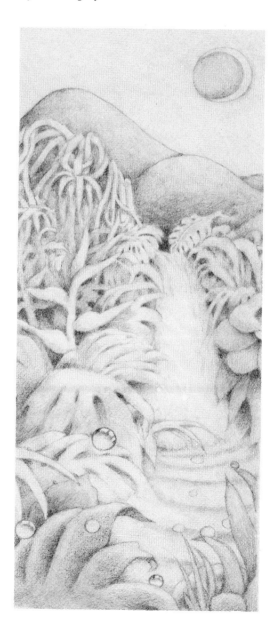

Scene Meditation

In this adventure, you step into a scene from your dreams and allow yourself to see, hear, smell, and feel everything within it. Then you explore this scene as a part of yourself.

Preparation

Pick a scene. (The definition of a scene is on page 29.)

Adventure

Close your eyes, breathe deeply, and relax . . . Gaze at your dream scene . . . Some of the details you will be asked to look for in this adventure will be details you remember clearly from the dream itself. Others you will have to create now, from your imagination.

Look carefully at what is happening in this scene . . . Imagine yourself walking all around it, looking at it. Notice the kind of light that exists here.

See the colors.

Listen, and hear the kinds of sounds you could hear here.

Imagine the kinds of smells you could smell.

Be aware of how you feel about this scene.

Take a look at any people you see. Note the ways in which these individuals project themselves — through dress, voice, gesture, action, presence . . . Look for anything striking that you can discover about them. Be aware of how you feel about them. Realize whether or not there is anyone else about to appear in this scene who hasn't yet arrived. If you feel that there is, try to sense who they are.

Then peek past the edges of this scene. See what is around the corner, over the next hill, or outside the window. Realize what environment surrounds this scene.

Now recognize the ways in which this scene reflects feelings you have been experiencing in your waking life. To do this, contemplate how you feel about this scene. Then think about times that you have felt similar feelings while you were awake. What other situations have triggered the kinds of feelings in you that this scene does? What do these situations mean to you? What has caused feelings like these to go away?

After you have realized the ways this scene illustrates some of your own feelings, consider whether those feelings are ones that need to be healed. If so, do you know what would help them to heal? On the other hand, if you think these are feelings that need to be enhanced in you, what could you do to help enhance them? To find out more about healing or enhancing these feelings, remember to ask for dreams that will give you more insights, before you go to sleep tonight.

Now take some slow, deep breaths. Feel the ways in which your dream scene and the feelings surrounding it are vibrant and alive within you. Then release the scene from your exclusive attention. Return your attention to your body and to the physical environment surrounding you . . . When you feel ready, blink and open your eyes.

The Union of Three Dream Characters

With this adventure, you can explore the essence of three characters and see how they relate to one another. You can also begin to
see these three characters as parts of yourself you are learning to
integrate.

Preparation

Pick three characters that you encountered in the same dream. Try
a writing, art, or movement adventure with each of these characters before you embark upon this adventure.

Adventure

Close your eyes and breathe deeply. Bring one of these three dream
characters into your focus. Notice how you respond to the presence
of this character.

Imagine yourself walking around this character, perceiving
this character with all of your senses. Then position yourself so that
you can gaze into this character's eyes. If this is a character that did
not have eyes in the dream, imagine these eyes now. What do the
eyes look like? Gaze into them and recognize this character's spirit
reflected there. Understand this character's deepest desire.

Then imagine yourself touching this dream character. If this
character is a person, you might want to try touching hands. Pay
attention to the sensations you feel when you touch.

When you feel that you have become acquainted with this
character's spirit, breathe deeply and bring the next dream character you have chosen to explore into your focus. Repeat this same
meditation with this new character. Then go ahead and embark
upon this meditation with the last dream character you picked.

Now that you have familiarized yourself with each of these three characters individually, bring all three characters into your focus at the same time. Let the images of these three characters overlap. Allow them to mingle and dance with one another. As they interweave, begin to see what these characters are telling you about their relationship to one another. Now allow these characters to transform each other.

Imagine them blending together into one image. See the way the union of these three characters looks.

Recognize what you can learn from the union of these three characters. Can you see these three characters as different parts of yourself that need to grow together? What would happen if you blended these three parts of yourself together in your life? What new phase of growth would you move into? How might this blending enhance your own ability to share love in your life? Take as much time as you need to contemplate these questions . . .

When you feel that you have learned as much as you can from these three characters and their union with one another, thank each of these dream characters individually and release them from your focus.

Then breathe deeply and return your attention to the sensations in your body. Hear the noises in your surroundings. Remind yourself of the physical environment of which you are a part. Feel what is around you. When you feel ready, and not before, open your eyes softly. Gently return your attention to your waking world.

Expanded Self Meditation

This adventure will help you get in touch with your Expanded Self. In other words, it can guide you to your deepest truth, the essence of who you are.

Preparation

To participate in this adventure, you must find an Expanded Self dream character to explore. Expanded Self characters are usually images that seem awesome to you in some way. Most often they are images that impress you either by their strength, their beauty, their wisdom, their mirth, their intensity, or their magical qualities.

Remember that deep blue lake you once saw in your dreams? That was a reflection of your own expanded awareness. Other examples of Expanded Self dream characters might include a sparkling, green jewel, a huge, old grey walrus, a big, strong mountain woman who moves boulders, a purple and blue butterfly, a little, white-haired man with wise, old eyes, or an image of yourself flying high above the treetops.

If you feel that you need more information about the Expanded Self before you begin this adventure, turn to the Expanded Self Writing adventure on page 112. Otherwise, look at your dreams and find one of these characters.

Adventure

Lie down and close your eyes. Breathe from the roots of your being, slowly and deeply . . . Be aware of the way that your body feels right now, without judgment . . .

Be aware of the places where your body touches the floor. Feel how the floor supports you . . . Be aware of those places where some parts of your body contact other parts of your body . . . Be aware of those places where your skin touches the air . . .

Now imagine your Expanded Self character in front of you. Perceive this character with all of your senses. Feel its presence. Breathe deeply and take in the essence of this character.

Now imagine that all around you — two inches out from your skin, in every direction — you are surrounded by the presence of your Expanded Self character. Feel this character's energy all around you . . . You may sense this energy as light . . . You may hear it as sound . . . You may feel it as warmth and peacefulness settling around you . . . Or you may recognize the presence of your Expanded Self in some other way . . .

Be aware of this energy surrounding you completely. Gently breathe the energy of the Expanded Self in with each inhalation . . . and with each exhalation, let go of any blocks to this energy . . . Let it fill you. Feel warmth spreading through your stomach, your chest area, and all around your heart as you breathe this energy into yourself . . .

Know that this Expanded Self energy is now both within you and around you. Let yourself be deep and full. Be at one with your Expanded Self . . .

Now ask yourself to remember any other images you might have seen or beings you might have encountered recently — either in waking life or dreams — that were reflections of this same Expanded Self energy . . . Notice any images, sounds, or feelings that come to mind when you make this request. Take as much time as you need to do this.

Now ask yourself if there are any more forms in which you need to recognize your Expanded Self at this time. Notice any images, sounds, or feelings that come to mind when you make this request. Again, take as much time as you need to do this.

And then remember, once again, that the energy of your Expanded Self character is within you and around you. Breathe this energy in and out one more time, as deeply as you can.

Then when you feel ready, you can begin to release your focus on the Expanded Self. Yet remember, as you do so, that the Expanded Self character you just explored reflects your own energy, in an expanded form . . . it remains in you even as you remove your attention from it.

Now gradually move your attention to your skin. Feel the places where your skin touches the air . . . Take a gentle, deep breath. Notice the places where parts of your body touch other parts of your body, the places of contact . . . Take another deep breath.

Then be aware of the places where your body touches the floor. Feel how the floor supports you . . . Take one more deep breath now and then return to your natural breathing rhythm. Be aware of the way your body feels now . . .

Then when you feel ready, softly blink, breathe deeply, and open your eyes. Take some quiet moments to fully reenter your waking world.

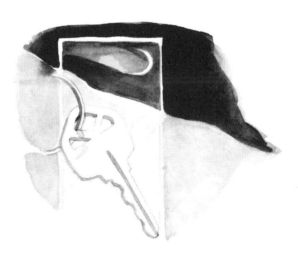

❧ *Advanced Movement Adventures* ❧

Continuous Movement

This adventure is an expanded version of the Basic Positions adventure, described on page 68. It is done with three characters instead of one, and ends up turning into a simple dance.

Preparation

Choose three dream characters.

Adventure

Find a body position for each of these characters, as described in Basic Positions on page 68. After you have completed all three, return to the position you chose for the first of these three characters. As soon as you are in this position, begin to move slowly and gently into the position you chose for the second character.

Once you are in this position, move into the position you chose for the third character. And when you have moved into this third position, let this position transform into the first position again. Move from one position to the next with slow, continuous, Tai Chi-like movements. Pay particular attention to the transitions or shifts that take place in you as you move from one position to another. Repeat this continuous cycle of three movements at least five times.

Then, as you go through the cycle of movements again, notice whether any of the movements want to expand, becoming bigger or stronger. Notice too, whether these movements want to transform each other and blend with each other in any way. If you feel like your movements want to change and blend with one another, let them do so. Repeat this new dance at least three times.

Then gently bring your movements to a halt and release these characters from your focus. Breathe deeply.

Sit down and contemplate these three characters as parts of yourself. Consider the ways that these three parts of you can work together and strengthen one another.

Acting out a Dream Suggestion

Now it's time to be really experimental. Play with this adventure and you will see your dreams transform your waking life in new, creative ways.

Preparation

Find an image or part of an image from your dreams with which you could make contact in physical reality. Here are some examples of ways you could do this.

- If you dreamed of the color blue, you could wear blue the following day or lie outside in the grass and contemplate the blue sky.

- If you dreamed of someone you know in waking life, you could tell this person about your dream, or just invite this person over to tea so that you can talk and discover what the two of you have to share.

- If you dreamed that you saw yourself playing the piano — something you've never done before in waking life — you could either go visit a friend who has a piano and try playing around on it, or you could decide to sign up for piano lessons.

Adventure

Make contact with your dream image in physical reality in whatever way you choose. Be innovative!

☙ *Ten-Day Dream Journey* ☙

The following pages contain a ten-day outline of suggested dream adventures for the more seasoned dream traveller. When you have explored many of the adventures in Chapter Four or done the basic dream journey described there, then I would say you are ready for this one.

You will find that this journey contains both "basic" adventures from Chapter Four, which are marked by a "B," and "advanced" adventures from this chapter, which are marked by an "A." The number of stars by each adventure indicate how many characters you will explore with that adventure. For instance, in Day 1, the three stars (☆☆☆) by "Informal Haiku" indicate that you need to explore three characters through that adventure. The lack of stars by "Dream Circles" indicates that that adventure does not involve the use of characters.

Please note that in Day 8, I ask you to explore a day in your waking life rather than a nighttime dream.

Suggested Adventures

Day 1

Dream Circles: A

☆☆☆ Informal Haiku: A

Day 2

Themes: B

☆☆ Art in Combination with Haiku: A

Day 3

Acting Out a Dream Suggestion: A

☆ Character Description: A

☆ Dream Character's Home (use the same character as you did in the adventure listed above): A

Day 4

Acting Out a Dream Suggestion: A

☆☆☆ Continuous Movement: A

☆☆☆ Union of Three Dream Characters (work with the same three characters you explored in the adventure listed above): A

Day 5

Scene Meditation (choose one scene to explore, rather than any characters): A

Scene Description (with the same scene): A

Either Dream Pillowcases or Scene in a Shoebox (with the same scene you explored in the above two adventures): A

Day 6

☆ Dialoguing: B

☆ Character Description: A

☆☆ Mandala (with the same two characters you explored in the adventures listed above): A

Day 7

Themes: B

☆☆☆ Hand Movements: B

Theme Free Association: A

Day 8

Record the events of a day in your waking life.

Themes: B

☆ Basic Positions: B

☆ Free Association Art: B

☆ Informal Haiku: A

Theme Free Association: A

Day 9

☆ Expanded Self Meditation: A

☆ Basic Positions (with the same Expanded Self Character): B

☆ Expanded Self Writing (with the same Expanded Self character): A

Day 10

☆ Basic Positions (with the Expanded Self character): B

☆ Expanded Self Writing (with the same character): A

☆ Masks (with the same Expanded Self character): A

7

Exploring Dreams in a Group

Choosing to honor our dreams and make changes in our lives so that we can explore our dream images is not always easy. Part of the reason for this is that we lack a modern cultural tradition that encourages us to make dream exploration a vital part of our daily lives. Without the kinds of group rituals many tribal societies have engaged in that focused on "the dreamtime," we often feel that we don't have much support for delving into our dreams.

Yet our culture is also, currently, in the midst of a great period of growth, when all of this is beginning to shift. More and more of us are realizing that we are spinning a dry wheel at a time when we need to go and find out why the riverbeds have no water. And more and more of us are willing to reach out and hold each other gently in our hearts and minds as we nurture each other's desire to expand.

So, when you recognize the need for help with your dream journey, reach out to other dreamers. Gather some friends and acquaintances together, or advertise for individuals interested in forming a dream group. Investigating your dreams with other people can be a delightful learning process. It will make you laugh at times, challenge the compassion within you, and ultimately help you to reawaken the love within yourself.

Often, in the classes I have taught, someone has recounted a dream and the rest of us have dissolved in mirth. On other occasions, someone has shared a dream and the apparent grace and resiliency of that person's spirit has brought tears to our eyes. By sharing our dreams together, we have allowed each other to see our secret fears, our silliness, our most delicate hopes, and our clearest visions. At the same time, we have also offered each other glimpses of the strength, beauty, and humor that lie at the core of our beings.

Your dreamsharing can be a precious gift exchange, too. The instructions given at the beginning of this chapter can help you get your dream group moving in this direction. If you would like more specific guidelines for your group's explorations, turn to one of the Dream Group Journeys beginning on page 185. There you will find a suggested schedule of adventures to try over a period of ten weeks.

Then move forward and discover your shared journey . . . As you explore new dimensions together, you will transform your world in a warm, positive way.

Setting up a Dream Group

● *Meeting times.* You will probably want to meet once a week for two to three hours, or more than once a week, if you have a really gung-ho group.

● *Ten-week group commitment.* Ask each person to make a commitment to the group for approximately ten weeks. Journeying together for this length of time will help group members to become familiar with each other and more relaxed about sharing personal feelings.

● *A group facilitator.* Choose a facilitator or leader to guide the group. This person can help the group to focus on the adventures at hand, set a time limit on them, and make sure that no individual in the group monopolizes sharing time. If you like, you can alternate facilitators from week to week.

● *Sensitivity.* Sometimes the temptation to define someone else's dream images becomes very strong. We have a brilliant interpretation of another person's dream that we know is "right" and we want to share it with them. However, your facilitator should remind the group that each of you needs to unfold the meaning of your own dreams. We can gently describe the relationships we see within another's dreams, but we cannot push our analysis of those relationships on the dreamer. Each of us must discover the meaning of our dreams in our own, unique way.

● *Confidentiality.* Your facilitator should also state that all information shared within the group needs to remain confidential. Dreams shared during the meeting should not be recounted outside the group. When everyone agrees to honor this request, a greater sense of trust can grow between all group members and the process of sharing will be more fun.

- *An "art box."* If you wish to enter into any dream/art adventures as a group, you will need to collect a box full of materials that could be used in art projects. For suggestions about the kinds of items you might want to include in your box, turn to the description of the art box on page 30. Then get a good-sized box from the grocery store and ask each member of your group to bring in at least one item to donate to a shared art box, as well as scissors and glue.

- *Preparation for the first week.* Everyone should skim over the first three chapters of this book. This will give you all a shared point of departure for your group journey.

- *Terms.* You will all need to know what a "character" and a "scene" are, before embarking on any of these adventures. Those definitions begin on page 28.

- *Suggested journeys.* If you would like to follow specific guidelines for a ten-week dream exploration as a group, turn to one of the dream group journeys described at the end of this chapter.

Sharing Individual and Partner Adventures

One of the best ways to work as a group is to work individually on some of the adventures in Chapters Four and Six and then have each person share their experiences with the group afterwards. You can work on a writing or art adventure, or have your facilitator read one of the meditation or movement adventures aloud, while you each participate.

Another wonderful way to work is to divide up into pairs and do some of the partner adventures in Chapter Nine. I highly recommend Point of View, Verbal Dialoguing, Body and Spirit, and Partner Meditations.

❧ *Verbal Group Adventures* ❧

These adventures are designed to be done out loud, with more than one person. Many of them are adaptations of individual or partner adventures described in other chapters.

Group Free Association

In this adventure, your group chooses a theme, and then creates a waking dream together, based on this theme.

Preparation

Pick a theme — either one that some in the group have been dreaming about, or one of those listed below.

Suggested Themes

Healing	Freedom
Wealth	Mastery
Tenderness	Growth
Birth	Trust
Death	Power
Challenges	Family
Wisdom	Humor
Movement	Creativity
Home	Dreams

Adventure

This adventure must be read aloud to the group. The person who assumes this task should take a few minutes to look over the text before reading it aloud.

Find a comfortable spot in the room. Then close your eyes, breathe deeply, and relax. Take a few moments just to feel your own breathing . . . Now begin to focus on the theme of _____, that we have selected. When you feel ready, you can express aloud any images, messages, or sensations that come to you in relation to this theme . . .

(Give your group several minutes to do this.)

Feel free, at this time, to make any sounds or movements that you associate with this theme.

(Give your group a few minutes more to do this.)

Now silently dream the personal version of this theme, which is _____.

(Fill in the blank with the personal version of this theme, which begins with "I" or "my," as in the list below. As you can see, the theme of "healing" becomes either "I heal" or "my healing." A theme such as "wealth" simply becomes "my wealth.")

I heal	My freedom
My wealth	I master
My tenderness	I grow
My birth	I trust
I die	My power
My challenges	My family
My wisdom	My humor
I move	I create
My home	I dream

(Give your group several minutes to do this.)

Next, make any sounds or movements that you feel represent the personal version of this theme.

(After group members have had several minutes to experience this, begin the third part of this adventure by choosing an image from the list below.)

Now I would like one of you to tell us more about this same theme by describing the _____ that you feel reflects this theme.

(Fill in the blank with one of the images from the following list. For example, if the theme the group is exploring is "I heal," you might ask one of your group to describe the cave that he or she visualizes as a symbol of the words "I heal." When this person is finished, ask another person to describe the outfit of clothing that he or she feels is representative of the words "I heal." Continue in this way, until everyone in the group had a turn describing the theme with an image.)

Suggested Images

cave	vehicle
body of water	living room
language	mountain
forest	building
sky	school
toy	time of day
plant	animal
meal	outfit of clothing
town	

Now that everyone has had a turn to explore this theme, each of you can breathe deeply and quietly release this theme from your focus . . . Return your attention to your own body and take five slow, deep breaths . . . Then gently open your eyes.

Take time to anchor some of the images that came to you during this adventure, by writing them down.

Now we can go on and engage in one of the Basic Dream Adventures in Chapter Four, as a way of exploring the messages in these images.

Picking up the Thread

Using this lively, verbal, group version of the Themes adventure, you can begin to see patterns within each other's dreams. Remember that it is *patterns* you are looking for here — not specific interpretations of each other's images. If you have a question about a certain image, remember to ask the dreamer to describe their feelings about that image.

Preparation

Everyone reviews Themes on page 55 before coming to the group meeting. Then each of you selects a whole dream to explore, rather than a single character or scene. A dream containing multiple images is best.

If you like, you can break up into groups of three or four people at this point, and explore this adventure in small groups. (It's fun to engage in this adventure with a larger group, but this takes more time and energy. So choose whichever way works better for your group!)

Adventure

One of you shares a dream out loud with the group. Everyone listens carefully. Then this same person shares the dream again very slowly and any of you say "stop" whenever you notice any parallel, contrasting, or particularly strong images. After the person is done sharing the dream a second time, your group discusses the themes you were able to pick out.

Then everyone sits quietly and writes down several titles for this dream. After you have all shared your titles with the dreamer, another individual tells a dream out loud and your group repeats this adventure.

Show, Do, and Tell

To engage in this adventure, you get to do some "homework" individually and then share it with the group.

Preparation

Your group leader asks you to do the following homework.

- Look for a physical object that is similar to one you saw in your dreams and bring this object to class.

- Find a way to bring one of your dream images in physical form. For instance, if you saw yourself dancing in a dream, you could spend some time dancing the next day. If you heard a certain song in your dreams, you could call your local radio station and request that song. If you dreamed about a certain person or place, you could go and see that person or place. After you have done this, come to the group prepared to talk about what you have done.

Adventure

Each of you shares the object you brought to class, and describes the dream in which you saw that object. Then each of you describes the dream image you "created" in physical reality and the dream from which that image came.

After this, you can share any insights that came to you about your object or image, as a result of making contact with this object or image in a physical way.

When every person in your group has participated, you can all enter into some dream adventures with the objects and images you shared. I recommend Dialoguing, Point of View, Free Association Writing, or Free Association Art from Chapter Four. You might also want to try Group Positions or Partner Meditations from Chapter Nine, using the objects that were brought in as the "characters" to explore.

❧ *Group Art Adventures* ❧

Dream Gifts

This adventure needs to be started during your first dream group meetings. It is a lovely way for you to express appreciation of one another during your shared dream journey.

Preparation

At the first or second group meeting, your group leader writes everyone's name on a slip of paper and puts these slips of paper in a hat. Everyone draws a name without revealing whose name it is. During the course of your ten weeks together, each of you pays particular attention to the dreams of the person whose name you have drawn.

Adventure

Buy and/or create a "dream gift" for the person whose name you have chosen, before your last group meeting. In classes I've taught in the past, a few people have bought items for one another like a button saying "think big" for the person whose dreams were full of reminders to stop underestimating themselves, some bubble bath for the person who was always dreaming of floundering about in water, or a paintbrush for the person who often dreamed about color or painting. Usually when people bought presents for one another, however, these were small items that accompanied homemade gifts.

Homemade gifts often resembled the products of the art adventures in this book — three dimensional creations made from "art box" materials. Sometimes they were miniature watercolor paintings, or special little "dream books" full of magazine images, drawings, and phrases based on the dreams of the person who was receiving the gift.

You can create your gifts in whatever way you like. However, the more elaborate your gifts are and the more closely they resemble the dreams of the person receiving them, the more fun your final group sharing will be. When your last group meeting arrives all too soon, remember to set aside plenty of time for sharing these gifts and the inspirations behind them. I promise you this will be a very special event.

Cartoons

Sometimes this adventure can get a small group of dreamers giggling nonstop — so beware! It's also a wonderful, light way to look at some options for creating a greater sense of harmony within ourselves.

Preparation

If your dream group has six or more people in it, separate into smaller groups of two, three, or four. Each of you collects paper and either a pen, pencil, or other sketching tools.

Then pick an image from your dreams in which you saw a strong conflict or contrast between two characters. A *conflict* is any image in which there is a strong sense of discomfort, fear, pain, disaster, or destruction (like two people arguing, someone breaking into your house, a big machine coming and chopping down a whole group of trees that you loved).

A *contrast* is any image where something unusual or unexpected is taking place, where opposites appear, or differing opinions or behaviors are expressed (like a couple dancing near a person who sits alone in a wheelchair, an opera singer singing on the steps of a big library, or a toilet affixed to the end of a dining room table).

Adventure

One of you shares a dream with the members of your small group and tells which conflict or contrast you have chosen to explore.

Your group identifies the two sides of the conflict or contrast. As you do this, you might also want to discuss with the dreamer what two desires, feelings, or purposes are really conflicting or contrasting here. Now all of you prepare to create cartoons based on this conflict or contrast.

Each of you draws a rectangle on your paper and divides it into three good-sized boxes, big enough to put a cartoon image in each box. Then you place an image that represents one side of the conflict or contrast in your first box.

In the second box, create an image that represents the second side of the conflict or contrast.

In the third box, create an image that represents one way of integrating or harmonizing the two different sides of the contrast or conflict.

These cartoons can be abstract, containing designs or patterns that represent the essence or underlying feeling of each side of the contrast or conflict. Or they can be more story-like, containing images of the actual characters involved in the dream and the sort of conversation they might have had. This method can often be more humorous.

When each of you has made a cartoon representing the dream, you can all share your cartoons with the dreamer. Then the next person in your group shares a dream and this adventure continues until all of you have had cartoons made for you.

For instance, one person in your group might share a conflict image from a dream in which a big machine came and chopped down a whole cluster of trees this person loved.

Your group would first identify the two sides of the conflict — "the machine" and "the trees" — and then ask the dreamer about the two conflicting desires, feelings, or purposes that these images represented. The purpose symbolized by the machine might be "to create a greater sense of order" or "to achieve certain goals and to destroy anything that seems like it might get in the way of those goals" . . . or something like that. The feeling represented by the trees might be "love itself," "a love of all things natural and beautiful," or "the desire to honor one's own natural beauty and style of growth . . ."

After listening carefully to the discussion of these images, each of you would draw three boxes on your paper. In the first box, you would draw a symbol of the machine or the purpose behind the machine.

In the second box, you would draw a symbol of the trees or the feelings reflected by the trees.

Then in the third box, you would draw a symbol of the integration of this dreamer's two conflicting desires or purposes . . . In this case, the integration symbol would probably be one that represented a way that the dreamer could have a sense of organization and goal achievement while also honoring what they love . . .

Note: To deepen this adventure and make it easier, each of you could do Dialoguing with your two conflict characters and share these dialogues with each other before you draw the cartoons.

Haiku and Artwork

This adventure combines simple writing and artwork. It is also a special way for individuals in the group to give gifts to one another.

Preparation

Before your group does this adventure, I suggest that you look over Informal Haiku on page 96 and Themes on page 55, for an understanding of parallels and contrasts.

If your dream group consists of six or more people, separate into smaller groups of three or four and place the art box in a location that is accessible to all the groups. Each of you needs to collect a pen, a plain sheet of paper, and a piece of construction paper.

Then each of you selects a dream and three characters from that dream you would like to explore.

Adventure

One of you shares your dream with the small group. Everyone in the group, including the "dream sharer," then looks for parallels and contrasts in this dream and discusses some of the relationships or themes going on within it. The person sharing the dream tells the group which three characters from this dream he or she has chosen to explore.

All of you write three haiku (or short, simple poems) on the plain sheet of paper — one for each of the three characters.

Then fold the construction paper into three equal sections. Copy one of the haiku into one of the sections on the front of the paper, and the other two haiku into two of the sections on the back.

Next, turn back to the haiku you wrote for the first dream character. In one of the empty sections next to this haiku, put colors, shapes, textures, or symbols that remind you of this character. (Materials for this can be found in your art box.)

In one of the other empty sections, go ahead and place colors, shapes, symbols, and textures that remind you of the second dream character. Put your artistic impressions of the third dream character in the last remaining empty section. When your group has finished this last bit of artwork, each of you should have a completed project that looks something like this:

One side			Other side		
artwork for the first character	haiku for the first character	artwork for the second character	haiku for the second character	artwork for the third character	haiku for the third character

Each of you shares your completed haiku and artwork and presents it to the dreamer. Then your group continues this adventure, creating haiku and artwork for the next person's dream.

Puppets

In this adventure, you explore a dream conflict using puppets you have made.

Preparation

Your group leader takes out the art box before the group does this adventure and makes sure that it has some of the following puppet materials in it.

If members of your group want to make finger puppets, you will need cloth, rubber bands, crayons, and glue. If the group members want to assemble puppets on a stick, you will need either popsicle sticks or twigs, and glue. And if individuals in your group want to get really elaborate and create painted papier-mâché puppets, you will need some balloons, material for papier-mâché, and paint.

When all the materials are gathered for this adventure, your group forms small groups of three or four people. All of you look at your own dreams and find a conflict between two characters you would like to explore. A *conflict* is any situation in the dream in which there was strong discomfort, unhappiness, fear, pain, sickness, or destruction.

Adventure

Each of you creates puppets to represent the two characters involved in your own dream conflict. Next, take turns using your puppet characters to act out your conflict situation. As you do this, allow your puppet characters to express what they are feeling about the situation.

Then act out the dream situation once again, only this time consider the ways in which your puppet characters' interactions would change, if both characters worked to create a more harmonious relationship with one another. Show your puppet characters beginning to resolve their conflict and expressing their responses to this resolution.

When your puppet show is complete, you and your group can discuss the experience and what it taught you about the resolution of this dream conflict.

After this, the next person in your group does a puppet show and this adventure continues until everyone in the group has performed a little show.

Note: Here are some suggestions of ways to make puppets. If your group is doing finger puppets, each of you draws the two characters onto different pieces of cloth, glues other materials onto these basic designs, and then attaches the finished puppets to different fingers using rubber bands. If your group is making puppets on a stick, each of you creates characters by gluing different materials onto the tops of popsicle sticks or twigs.

If your group is making fancy papier-mâché puppets, blow up two balloons apiece and cover them almost completely with papier-mâché, leaving a small opening at the bottom of each balloon. When the papier-mâché is dry, pop your balloons and paint the papier-mâché shells to look like the dream characters you are exploring.

❧ *Group Movement Adventures* ❧

Group Positions

This is a meditative way for each group member to explore a dream character, with the assistance of the whole group.

Adventure

Your group divides up into small groups of approximately four people each. (However, you can embark upon this adventure as a whole group if you have the time and energy to do it that way.)

One of you describes a dream out loud and then chooses a character from that dream you'd like to explore. The rest of you can ask questions to clarify the nature of this character.

Then each of you, including the dreamer, spreads out in the room and puts your body in a unique position that feels to you as though it represents the essence of this character. The position you choose doesn't have to mimic the character, it just has to feel the same way that the character feels to you.

To help you with this, your facilitator asks you to consider whether the position feels like it needs to be low to the ground or up high, rounded or angular, hard or soft, active or passive, strong or weak, and so on.

When each of you has found a body position and has had a moment or two to experience the position, the leader asks, "How does this position feel to your body? . . . Is there tension somewhere in your body? . . . Is there an increase of energy in any part of the body, as it resides in this position? . . . Does your body recognize this position in any way?" Everyone takes some time to contemplate each of these questions.

Then any of you who would like to make sounds that remind you of this character can do so.

When the sounds have died away, you can start pretending that you are this dream character, that the spirit of this character lives in you. Each of you begins to move in a way that you feel represents the essence of this character.

Then any of you can express any feelings out loud, that you experience as this character. One of you might say something like, "I feel boxed in," and someone else might add, "Yes, but I feel safe." Continue taking turns sharing your impressions of what it feels like to be this character, for several minutes. Then your facilitator gently instructs all of you to release this character from your focus and return your attention to your own bodies and your own spirits. Each of you gradually opens your eyes and returns to a group circle, when you feel ready to discuss your experiences with this adventure.

After a brief discussion, continue this adventure with another person's dream character, until everyone has had a turn.

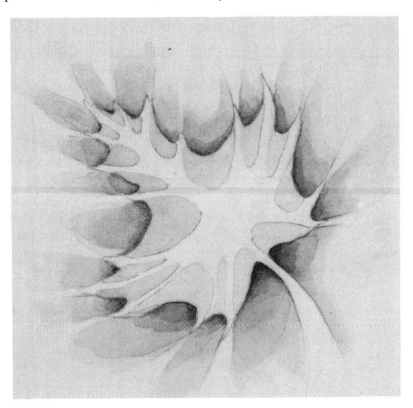

Dream Dance

This adventure can be as elaborate as you wish to make it.

Preparation

Divide into small groups. Choose a theme your group would like to explore together. You can make up one of your own, or choose one of those listed below.

Suggested Themes

Maleness	Confinement
Femaleness	Release
Music	Children
Water	Leadership
Cleanliness	Oldness
Time	Shopping
Vulnerability	Nakedness
Disguises	Aggression
Animal wisdom	Technology
Artistry	Friendship

Now, each of you finds three characters in your dreams that are related to this theme.

Adventure

Each of you explores Continuous Movement on page 147 with your three characters. (Basically this adventure involves finding a different body position for each of the three characters and then moving your body from one position to the next in a continuous flow of movement.)

You can engage in this adventure while remaining in fairly close proximity to each other, but you should stay attuned to your own movements, at first.

When you have all completed Continuous Movement a few times, each of you repeats your same movements, but starts to become increasingly aware of the movements of others in your group. Remain true to the basic nature of the movements you have developed on your own, while you begin to move in relationship to each other. Let your movements blend to some degree with those of others in your group. Transform each other's movements. Allow your movements to become a dance that incorporates aspects of the Continuous Movement each of you has created. You can make this dance as simple or as intricate as you like.

After the dance feels complete, you can all talk about your dance and discuss what you learned from it.

Acting and Transforming

In this active adventure, you pool your creative resources to help each individual in your group explore a dream and transform it in a powerful way.

Preparation

Each of you selects a whole dream to explore. Then one of you needs to volunteer to be the "dreamer," three to five of you need to be "actors," and the rest of you will be "the audience."

Adventure

Preparing to Act out the Dream

Dreamer: Share a dream, then choose a "role" by picking one of the characters in the dream that you would like to play. This time you can play yourself, if you like.

Actors: You choose roles from the dream, too. Remember you don't have to play a person — the character you play can be a distinctive tree or a road with a specific name. And one of you should agree to play "the dreamer" (as this person was portrayed in the dream), if the actual dreamer has not selected this role already. Now, before you act the dream out, go ahead and ask the dreamer any questions you have about the character you are going to play. When you are acting your character out, you will be expressing how you feel as the dream character you are portraying . . . so get a good sense of this character now!

Audience: Be attentive, and give helpful feedback whenever it is needed.

Acting out the Dream Sequence

Dreamer and Actors: Act out the dream sequence in which your characters played a role. Allow your characters to express their feelings out loud, during the sequence.

Dreamer: If you feel that the dream is being misrepresented at any point, stop the action and explain to the actors what needs to change.

Actors: Respect the integrity of the dreamer and alter your character portrayal if you are asked to do so.

Transforming the Sequence

Dreamer: When the sequence has been completely acted out, consider whether or not you felt any conflict in this dream. If you did, ask the other actors to reenact the dream in a new way, creating a greater sense of resolution within it.

Actors: As you reenact the dream, make whatever changes in your characters' actions and responses you feel would help to bring the events of the dream sequence to resolution.

Dreamer: If you do not feel good about the resolution you and your fellow actors have created, ask the other actors to reenact the sequence with you once again, this time coming to resolution in a different way.

Discussion

Everyone talks about the dream sequence and your transformation of it. When you have completed this, a different person in your group will share a dream and you can begin this adventure with a new dream.

Dream Description

One of my students, named Heather, dreamed that she went to the Concord Public Library to see the picture of Henry David Thoreau that she knew was stored there. She glimpsed the picture in the back room as she came in, but when she talked to the librarian, the librarian refused to let her anywhere near it. Heather submitted to the librarian's will and withdrew, feeling helpless. When we selected roles from this dream, Heather chose to be the librarian and the other actors played the Concord Public Library, the picture of Henry David Thoreau, and Heather. They acted the dream out in the following manner.

Library: Here comes Heather . . . she is feeling a special vibrancy inside, I can tell. There is someone or something she loves here, that she means to make contact with . . . I am big, strong, and solid and am glad that she is going to find what she loves inside me.

Picture: It is me she is here for . . . my love! I exist for her as a symbol of inspiration . . . I want to go home with her, where I will be appreciated. With her help and support, I might be able to step out of my frame and live beyond these boundaries . . .

Heather *(to the librarian)*: May I please see the picture of Henry David Thoreau you have in the back room?

(The librarian looks "busy" and glances up from her books only briefly.)

Librarian: No. That picture is historical and must be carefully preserved for the public welfare. Only librarians can go back there and see it.

Picture: Here I am, Heather! Over here!

Heather: I see you! *(Then, to the librarian)* Ma'am, may I please go over and look at the picture?

Librarian *(raising her voice a little)*: No! You are not allowed to!

(Heather looks defeated and steps back. This version of the sequence is over. Now the actors reenact the sequence, attempting to bring it to resolution.)

Library: Here comes Heather. She looks expectant, glowing, as though she is coming to find someone or something she loves. Maybe she needs to know that she has support in this. I will help her now if I can.

Picture: Here comes my beloved. I hope she will claim me and take me home . . . that she will believe I am hers. I don't belong here amidst dust and disinterest. I am meant to inspire people . . . and I am not playing that role here. Heather would let me inspire her, and that would feel good. Oh, I will try and go with her this time!

Heather *(to the librarian)*: May I please see the picture of Henry David Thoreau you have in the back?

Librarian: No. It is put away, being preserved for posterity. Only librarians can go near it.

Heather: Please?

Librarian: No! I said no and I meant no! *(She glares at Heather coldly.)*

Heather: I insist that you let me see it!

Librarian: NO. *(Heather looks defeated. Then suddenly the picture jumps up, runs over to her and throws itself in her arms.)*

Picture: Quick, Heather, take me with you! I belong to you, not to someone else! Believe me! Take me with you now, quickly!

Library: He's right! He is yours! Here, run through my doors, I'll hold them wide open for you! Run with him, you are free! *(Heather and the picture run through the doors as the librarian's jaw drops open.)*

After this reenactment of the sequence was over, Heather admitted she'd been surprised by the resolution. Originally she thought the picture didn't belong to her, so that she must submit to the librarian's whims about whether she got to see it or not. Yet the other actors believed she needed to own the part of herself represented by the Thoreau picture and they helped her to claim it. Heather liked this idea. Later she did some Dialoguing with the picture, to find out more about this part of herself she'd been denying herself access to.

Dressing up as a Dream Character

This may be the craziest, most audacious adventure in this book. If your group is willing to be daring, no adventure will be as tantalizing as this one.

Preparation

Before you come to class, each of you chooses a dream character you would like to explore. Then all of you come to class dressed as the dream character you have picked.

Adventure

Take turns sharing the dream in which you found your dream character and telling the group your feelings about this character.

Next, each of you explores your character using an "individual" adventure, like Dialoguing, Basic Positions, or Body and Spirit, from Chapter Four. When you have all finished, each of you can share the information you learned through these adventures with the rest of the group.

Then prepare to spend some time acting your characters out. Each of you will move and talk as you feel your characters would do, throughout the rest of the evening. If your group is really brave, you might want to try going out in public as your characters. Go to an ice cream parlor, restaurant, or bar. Pretend to be your characters the whole time you are there. Each of you should speak as your characters would speak, gesture as your characters would gesture, and eat and drink as your characters would eat and drink.

If you don't want to go out, you can stay in your meeting place and all pretend to be in an environment like a mountain meadow, a store, or a classroom. Once again, remember to act as your character would act in each situation.

When you stay in character for an hour or so, you can increase your understanding of this dream character and of the part of you it represents. You might also discover that you don't want to come out of character!

After you have all given yourselves time to enjoy this experience, you can end the evening . . . Then the following week each of you can share any new insights you gained into ways that this character is a part of you.

◦ *Beginning Dream Group Journey* ◦

This ten-week journey, designed for a beginning dream group, is similar to the journey I teach in my introductory dream classes. I suggest that you use it as a guide in composing your own dream group journey.

Before every group meeting, each of you should choose one dream to explore, except in Week 8, when you will be exploring one day in your waking life as if it were a dream.

The number of stars by each adventure indicates the number of dream characters to explore with that adventure. For instance, in Week 1, since there is just one ☆ by the adventure called Partner Meditation, you would explore only one character through this adventure. Yet in Week 4, since there are three stars (☆☆☆) by Hand Movements, you would explore three characters in that adventure. (If you need to be reminded of the definition of a character, turn to Chapter Three and go over that definition.)

Please note that the adventures with a "G" after them are group adventures that can be found in this chapter. Those with a "B" after them are individual adventures that can be found in Chapter Four, called Basic Dream Adventures. Those with an "A" after them are individual adventures that can be found in Chapter Six, called Advanced Dream Adventures. And those with a "P" after them are partner adventures, found in Chapter Nine.

Suggested Adventures

Week 1

Discuss what dreams mean to each of you and what some of your most striking dreams have been.

> Begin Dream Gifts: G
>
> Group Free Association: G
>
> ☆ Free Association Writing: B
>
> ☆ Partner Meditation: P
>
> Sharing

Note: Ask everyone to do Show, Do, and Tell at home, so that you can share your experiences with this adventure at next week's meeting.

Week 2

> Show, Do, and Tell (sharing): G
>
> ☆ Point of View with a Partner: P
>
> ☆ Free Association Art: B
>
> ☆ Partner Meditation (if time allows): P
>
> Sharing

Week 3

> ☆ Point of View with a Partner: P
>
> ☆ Verbal Dialoguing: P
>
> ☆ Gift Exchange Meditation and Gifts (with the same character): B
>
> Sharing

Week 4

☆☆   Body and Spirit: P

☆☆☆ Hand Movements (with the two characters you've already explored in Body and Spirit and a third character from the same dream): B

Sharing

Note: Ask everyone to read Themes on page 55 as homework for next week's meeting. (This is preparation for the Picking up the Thread adventure you will do next week.)

Week 5

Picking up the Thread: G

☆   Body and Spirit: P

☆☆☆ Continuous Movement (with the character you just explored in Body and Spirit and two other characters from the same dream): A

Sharing

Note: Ask everyone to come to next week's meeting dressed like a dream character, in preparation for the adventure called Dressing up as a Dream Character: G.

Week 6

This week you will explore the character as whom you have dressed.

☆   Dressing up as a Dream Character: G

Note: As part of this adventure, do Body and Spirit: G with your character. Then either go out on the town to an establishment such as a restaurant or bar, walk around the town, or stay in your meeting place and all pretend to be in a given environment such as a grocery store, a mountain meadow, or a classroom. Act as your dream characters would act in each situation. At the end of the evening, discuss what you have learned from the part of yourself your character represents.

Week 7

Picking Up the Thread: G

☆ Dialoguing: B

☆☆ Cartoons (do this adventure with the character you dialogued with and its contrasting character): G

Sharing

Note: Ask everyone to write down the events of a day in waking life that occurs during the next week, and bring this to next week's meeting.

Week 8

Embark upon these adventures with the events of your day.

Picking Up the Thread: G

☆ Point of View with a Partner: P

☆ Body and Spirit: P

☆ Sharing

Note: Please remind everyone that they will be giving dream gifts in two weeks to the person whose name they drew in Week 1.

Week 9

Pick one Expanded Self dream character (as described in Expanded Self Writing on page 112).

☆ Expanded Self Meditation: A

☆ Expanded Self Writing: A or Dream Character's Home: A (The first of these is a writing adventure and the second is an art adventure, so choose whichever you prefer.)

☆ Group Positions (with this Expanded Self character): G

Sharing

Note: Ask everyone to read over Informal Haiku: A in preparation for next week's Haiku and Artwork adventure. Remind everyone that you are exchanging dream gifts next week.

Week 10

Complete Dream Gifts: G

☆☆☆ Haiku and Artwork: G

☆ Group Positions with one of the three characters you have already explored (if time allows): G

Last Sharing

❧ *Advanced Dream Group Journey* ❧

The following pages contain a ten week outline of suggested dream adventures for a group of more seasoned dream travellers. (This means that I recommend going on the beginning journey together before you embark on this one.)

Each week you will explore one dream. The number of characters you will explore from this dream are listed along with the adventures. The number of stars by each adventure indicate how many of these characters you will explore with that adventure. Please note that in Week 8, I ask you to explore a day in your waking life rather than a nighttime dream.

Remember that those adventures with a "B" after them come from Chapter 4: Basic Dream Adventures, those with an "A" after them come from Chapter 6, those with a "G" after them come from this chapter, and those with a "P" after them come from Chapter Nine.

Suggested Adventures

Week 1

Dream Gifts: G

Picking Up the Thread: G

☆☆☆ Haiku and Artwork: G

Sharing

Week 2

Dream Circles: B

☆ Body and Spirit: P

☆☆☆ Haiku and Artwork (include the character you explored in the preceding adventure as one of the three): G

Sharing

Note: Ask everyone to bring in either a shoebox or a washed white pillowcase next week.

Week 3

This week you pick a "scene" to explore, rather than characters. (A scene is described in Chapter Three.)

Scene Meditation: A

Scene Description (use the same scene or a different one): A

Dream Pillowcases or Scene in a Shoebox (use one of the scenes you explored in the adventures listed above): A

Sharing

Week 4

Choose two contrasting characters, as described in Cartoons: G.

☆ Body and Spirit: P

☆ Body and Spirit: P

☆☆ Cartoons or Puppets (with the two characters explored in the preceding adventures): G

Sharing

Week 5

Pick two contrasting or conflicting characters.

☆   Body and Spirit: P

☆   Body and Spirit: P

☆☆ Mandala and Mobile (choose either the Mandala or Mobile and explore the same two characters you have been working with so far): A

Sharing

Note: Please ask everyone to bring in a shoebox, or a box of similar size (no smaller than a shoebox) for next week's meeting.

Week 6

☆   Character Description: A

☆   Dream Character's Home: A

☆   Group Positions (do this group adventure with the same character you just explored): G

Sharing

Week 7

☆   Body and Spirit: P

☆☆☆ Dream Dance (include the character you explored in the Body and Spirit adventure as one of the three you work with in this adventure): G

☆☆☆ Union of Three Dream Characters (follow this adventure with the same three characters): G

Sharing

Note: Ask everyone to record the events of a day in their waking lives and to bring this to next week's meeting.

Week 8

Explore your waking day as if it were a dream, using the following adventures.

       Dream Circles: A (or Picking Up the Thread: G)

☆   Body and Spirit: P

☆☆☆ Dream Dance (including the character you explored in Body and Spirit as one of the three you explore in this adventure): G

☆☆☆ Union of Three Dream Characters (use the same three characters you just explored): A

       Sharing

Note: Please remind everyone that they will be giving dream gifts in two weeks to the person whose name they drew in Week 1.

Week 9

Select one Expanded Self character, as described in Expanded Self Writing, page 112.

       Acting and Transforming (use the dream in which you found the Expanded Self character): G

☆   Expanded Self Meditation: A

       Sharing

Note: Please remind everyone that they will be exchanging dream gifts next week.

Week 10

       Complete Dream Gifts: G

☆   Expanded Self Writing: A

☆   Group Positions (with the Expanded Self): G

       Sharing

Note: If your group would like to get together for one more special event, choose a time to share snacks and do Masks: A, with one of the Expanded Self characters you have already explored.

8

Dream Adventures for Children

Many of the adults I know who are interested in dreams today, loved their dreams as children and can still remember vibrant images from that time. I, on the other hand, had insomnia as a child and was terrified of my dreams. Often, when I lay in bed at night, I tried to convince myself that I wouldn't have to dream at all. "Just shut your eyes and the next thing you know, you'll be opening your eyes and it will be morning," I'd say to try to reassure myself.

I had no one to talk to about any of this. My mother did her best to comfort me when I padded into her room in the middle of the night, seeking comfort from another series of frightening images. She suggested that I think of nice things, like birthday parties. But there was no one with whom I could discuss my dream images themselves or my nightly ordeals of trying to convince myself to go to sleep.

I realize now how much it would have meant to me to have had someone there who could listen and guide me through those experiences. Thus, whenever one of my child friends shares their dreams with me today, I try to listen carefully. And I want to encourage you to do the same.

Whenever you take time to help a child explore their dreams, you give that little person a special gift. You help them affirm and express a part of their inner world. You teach them to honor the beauty within themselves.

For assistance in this magical sharing process, I suggest that you read over the first three chapters, gather an "art box" as described on page 30, and then start experimenting with some of the material in this chapter.

I have written the descriptions of these adventures as though I were speaking to a parent, yet you can still rely on them if you are a teacher, a relative, or a child's friend. Just keep in mind that you may have to adapt some of the ideas offered here to suit your child's needs and "inspirations of the moment." These adventures are guidelines only. Once you have actually embarked on your shared dream journey, both you and the child will probably discover some new directions you would like to go. Allow your imaginations to soar together.

Show Me and Tell Me about Your Dream

This is the most basic dream adventure to share with a child.

Adventure

Ask your child to share dreams with you. If your child tells you a dream right away, ask what he or she felt about different images in the dream. You might also want to encourage your child to draw a whole dream on paper. Then ask how your child feels about the drawn images.

Exchanging Gifts with Monsters and Friends

This dream adventure is a particularly good one to do with dream characters from one of two extremes — either those that really scare your child or those that seem especially friendly or affirmative.

Adventure

Ask your child to share a dream with you. Then pick one character from the dream. Remember that the characters who seem to play the strongest roles, or who seem to impress your child the most, are probably the best ones to use in this adventure.

Ask your child to imagine requesting a gift from this character. After he or she has done this, ask what the gift is. Next, suggest that your child imagine offering a gift to this character. Find out what this gift is.

Lastly, ask your child to create these gifts with the art materials you have gathered.

Special Dream Friends

This is a way of strengthening your child's confidence — of showing this small person acceptance, love, and support for being who they are.

Adventure

Whenever your child shares a dream with you in which he or she is doing an activity well, a favorite person, place, activity, or object appears, or a special dream friend comes forth — ask your child to draw this image on a big sheet of paper. Then hang this artwork up in a visible spot in your house or classroom, or over your child's bed or desk. (You can matte and frame the image, too, if you like.)

The next time your child has a conflict dream, help your young friend find a way to use this image, and the friendship or resources it represents, as an aid in dealing with the conflict.

Let's Draw a Happy Dream
out of a Scary One

This is a good adventure to engage in when your child has had a conflict dream or a nightmare. After your child has completed this adventure and redrawn the dream, you might put this picture on the wall or refrigerator as a reminder of his or her inner power.

Adventure

Ask your child to draw the whole dream. Then get a new sheet of paper. Tell your child you'd like to help make a happy dream out of that scary one. One of the following suggestions will help you do this.

- Ask your child to imagine having a friend who is very strong or who knows how to do magic and can "change things around." Then ask your child to redraw the dream with this special friend in the picture, helping to change the situation that was scary.

- Ask your child to pretend to have a magical tool, a gift from a great wizard, that can be used to change the situation in the dream. Then ask your child to redraw the dream showing how the use of this magical tool transforms the situation.

- Ask your child to pretend to be very big, strong, and capable of boldly stating feelings to the scary beings in the dream. Then ask your child to tell you how the dream changes once he or she has expressed these feelings clearly and directly. (Often if your child can imagine saying "no" strongly, the fear surrounding the dream will dissolve.) After having imagined the dream in this new way, ask your child to redraw the dream, showing how the dream situation is changed by this new ability to express feelings with confidence.

- Ask your child to pretend to ask the scary beings in the dream to be friends. If the little one has trouble with this, have the child ask the magical being, described above, to talk to the scary beings and request that they become the child's friends. Then ask the child to redraw the dream picture, showing the scary beings as friends.

You Pretend to Be Someone from Your Dream

This is "dialoguing" for kids!

Preparation

Help your child choose a dream character to explore. Those from one of two extremes — either special friends or monsters — are especially good characters for this adventure.

Adventure

Ask the child to pretend to be this dream character while you ask "this character" some questions. The following questions are some you might want to try. (Feel free to replace the words "my child" with your child's name.)

- Where do you live?
- What do you like to do the most?
- Do you have something you'd like to tell my child?
- Why do you do _____ in the dream? (Fill in the blank with the activity this character was participating in.)
- Can you be my child's friend?
- Can you help my child in some way? How?
- Can you please give my child a gift?
- My child would like to give you a present. What gift would you like to have?

If this character is one that scares your child, you might want to use this opportunity to make deals with the character. For example, you could say, "Okay, Madam Tiger, I'll let you out of the cage and bring you a special present, if you promise to be Jessie's friend. Will you promise that to Jessie?"

Continue this dialogue until you feel that you have helped your child to understand this character and have alleviated the fear your child experienced in the dream.

Let's Both Pretend

Generally, children love to act events out, so this dream adventure is an ideal one to engage in, especially after a nightmare. It is very similar to the "Let's Draw a Happy Dream out of a Scary One" adventure, only this one involves acting and that one involves drawing.

Preparation

Ask your child to share a dream with you.

Adventure

Each of you chooses different characters from the dream that you'd like to act out. (Other characters can be invisible — you can pretend that they're there.) Then act the dream out. One of the following suggestions might help you to do this.

- Ask your child to imagine having a friend who is very strong or who knows how to do magic and can "change things around." One of you will play the friend and the other will either be the child, or another character in the dream. Then reenact the dream, letting the special friend help to transform the frightening part of the dream.

- Ask your child to pretend to have a magical tool, a gift from a great wizard. Remind your child that this gift can be used to change the situation in the dream. Then reenact the dream, letting the child use this tool.

- Ask your child to pretend to be strong enough to change the situation in the dream either by clearly expressing feelings or by taking action to change the situation. (Often, if the child can imagine saying "no" strongly, the fearful atmosphere of the dream will dissolve.) Reenact the dream, letting the child change the situation using his or her own strength.

● Ask your child to pretend to ask the scary beings in the dream to be their friends. If your young friend has trouble with this, then tell the child to ask a magical being, like the one described above, to talk to the scary beings and request that they become the child's friends. Now suggest that the scary beings have a gift to give the child. Tell the child that the scary beings would like to receive a gift, too. Encourage the child to think of a gift to give them. When you reenact the dream, include this gift exchange as part of the re-enactment.

After you are done acting all this out, encourage your child to create these gifts, using art materials.

9

Dreamsharing with a Partner

When you agree to share dreams with another person, you are consenting to honor both "the eternal" and "the human" within that person. This is a very special, intimate experience. It can help you both awaken to the mystery of your own union and to the beauty of your own pulsing, unfolding beings.

The adventures described in the following pages can help you begin a dreamsharing experience with someone close to you. All of them are adventures that can be done in bed, when you wake up in the morning. Just remember to give yourselves time when you wake up — to go over your dreams individually and to jot down some notes — before you enter into these adventures. Then recognize that the road lies open before you. Some couples I've talked to who have shared dream journeys have actually begun dreaming together, in time. They see each other in their dreams, and when they wake up they remember having seen each other, and they recall similar dream images.

The kinds of discoveries you and your partner can make together in the dream state are endless. So gather up your dancing shoes, both of you, and head towards that open door. Follow your love into a new adventure.

Sharing Dreams Out Loud

This is the most basic way to share dreams with one another.

Adventure

Each of you takes a turn describing the previous night's dreams. In addition to describing the individual images in the dream, you might also want to take a look at any relationships you see between them. Then discuss the way you feel about some of the images.

Partner Meditation

This quiet adventure is a guided meditation that helps you delve deeply into one dream character and explore it with all of your senses and resources.

Adventure

One of you shares your dream with your partner and chooses a character within this dream to explore. When you are ready, your partner reads the following meditation to you, slowly and gently.

Note: You can replace the words "this character" with the name of the dream character throughout this adventure, if you like.

> Close your eyes . . . Breathe deeply . . . Allow yourself to slow down and relax . . . Take some time to experience your breath . . .
>
> Now imagine your dream character . . . Tell me the name of this character and a brief description of them . . . How do you respond to this character? Breathe and describe your response to me.
>
> Take another deep breath. Now locate this character in your body. Ask yourself, "Where do I feel this character in my body?" Pay attention to fleeting images and sensations. If you don't get an answer, take another deep breath, and ask again. Then tell me where this character is located in your body and how it feels here.
>
> Breathe deeply once again. Now imagine a color that seems related to this character. Ask yourself, "What color or colors reflect this character?" Notice all glimpses of color you see. When you have found the color which has the strongest relationship to this character, breathe this color in and out three times.
>
> If your dream character is disturbing to you in any way, imagine breathing a rainbow of colors in and out along with this color. Allow this color to flow in and out with

the others . . . Then tell me what the color is and how it affects you.

Take another deep breath. Now listen for a sound that seems related to this character. Ask yourself, "What sound do I associate with this character?" Notice all the fleeting noises, tones, or melodies you hear. When you have heard the sound, take three deep breaths and listen to it. Then tell me what the sound is and how you respond to it.

Now breathe deeply and ask yourself, "What smell reminds me of this character?" Take the time you need to recognize any scents or fragrances that pass through your awareness. Once you have found the smell, breathe it in and tell me your impressions of it. How do you feel about this smell?

Now allow yourself to experience this character in its entirety. Recognize the feelings this character brings up in you . . . the color . . . the sound . . . and the smell you associate with this character . . . Breathe deeply and contemplate the essence of this character . . . Then tell me any other insights that come to you about this character at this time.

Now breathe deeply and experience this character as part of yourself . . . Tell me the new role you think this part of you would like to play in your life.

Take a moment to absorb all that you have experienced in this adventure . . . Then release this character from your focus . . . As you do so, take a deep breath and feel it travelling through your body . . .

Take three more deep breaths. When you are ready, gently open your eyes and take the time you need to re-orient yourself to your surroundings.

Both of you can spend some time discussing this experience, if you like. Then switch roles and enter into this adventure again.

A Wealth of Meditation Adventures

Any of the meditation adventures in this book can be used by friends or lovers in the way that is described below.

Adventure

Take turns sharing your dreams out loud with one another. Then choose a meditation from one of the meditation sections in Chapters Four and Six. After you've found a meditation you both like, one of you lies down and closes your eyes, while the other person reads the meditation out loud.

When the meditation is complete, you can talk about the experience and then switch roles.

Point of View for Two

In this adventure, each of you takes a turn telling a dream out loud, from the point of view of one of your dream characters.

Preparation

One of you agrees to be "the dreamer," and the other "the listener."

Adventure

Dreamer

Share a dream and tell your partner which of the characters from that dream you would like to explore. Then pretend to be that character and retell the dream from the character's point of view. Allow yourself to *be* the dream character, and not just speak about the character. Tell everything that you saw and felt as this character, including anything that you notice from your new perspective that you didn't notice from your original dreaming perspective.

Listener

Absorb what "the dream character" says and ask this character any questions you have about the dream. For instance, you might ask, "Why did you climb that telephone pole?" or "How did you feel when that banana came flying through the window?"

Dreamer

When the listener has no more questions, release your focus from this character and return to a full awareness of your body and spirit.

Dreamer and Listener

After pausing to discuss this experience, change roles. This adventure is complete when each of you has told a dream from the point of view of one of the characters within that dream.

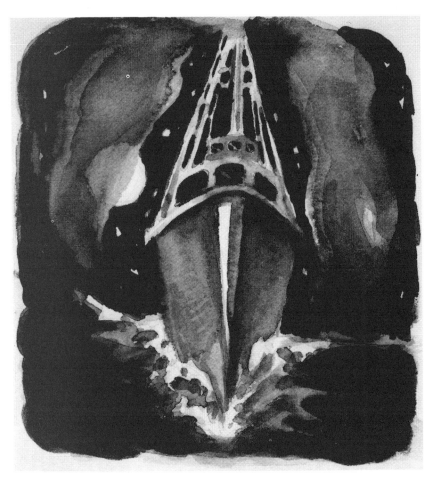

Verbal Dialoguing for Two

This adventure is a favorite in all my classes.

Preparation

One of you will start this adventure as "the dreamer," and the other as "the listener."

Adventure

Dreamer

Share a dream and tell your partner which character within that dream you would like to explore. Then close your eyes and breathe deeply . . .

Listener

Relax for a few moments with your partner. Then ask the dreamer to pretend to be this dream character . . . Encourage the dreamer to experience the character's energy and to see and feel as the character sees and feels.

Now tell the dreamer you are going to ask some questions. Remind the dreamer to respond to these questions as the dream character, using the word "I," when speaking for this character. Below are some questions you could ask. Feel free to add others!

- Who are you? How does it feel to be you?
- What knowledge do you have to share with the person who dreamed you?
- Why did you demonstrate your knowledge to this person in the way that you did?
- What part of this dreamer do you represent?
- Can you suggest any new actions for the dreamer to take in their waking lives?
- What do you have to tell the dreamer about new ways to grow and love?
- Is there anything else you wish to share with the dreamer at this time, or do you feel that this dialogue is complete for now?

When the dialogue is complete, instruct the dreamer to release this character's energy and to return to a full awareness of his or her own body and spirit. After pausing to discuss this experience, you can switch roles and continue this adventure.

Body and Spirit for Partners

This adventure is a combination of two powerful adventures —
Basic Positions and Verbal Dialoguing.

Preparation

One of you will start this adventure as "the dreamer," and the
other as "the listener."

Adventure

Dreamer

Share a dream and tell your partner which character within that dream you would like to explore. Then close your eyes, relax, and breathe deeply . . .

Now find a position in which to put your body that feels like it symbolizes your dream character. You do not have to imitate the way the character actually looked in the dream. Instead, find a position that feels the way the spirit or energy of this character feels to you.

Listener

When the dreamer has discovered a body position that represents the spirit of the dream character, you can begin asking the following questions. Instruct the dreamer to respond verbally to these questions and to answer as fully as they can.

Does this character's energy seem as though it is close to the ground, or up high?

Is the energy of this character heavy or light? . . . Hard or soft? . . . Active or passive? . . . Consistent or wavering? . . . Strong or weak? . . . Contracted or open? . . . Old or new?

Now pause and recognize how this body position feels to you. How does your body respond to this position? Is this a position that's familiar to your body in any way? Feel the energy of this character in your whole body, from your feet, up through your legs, torso, arms, neck, and head . . . Let yourself be filled with this character's energy.

Imagine that you are this character now . . . Answer the following questions directly as this character.

- How do you feel?

- Do you feel tension anywhere in your body?

- Is there some part of your body that feels like it is more vibrant than another part? . . . heavier than another part? . . . stronger than another part?

- Who are you?

- What do you have to tell the dreamer?

- Why do you try to reveal this information to them in the way that you did in the dream?

- What part of this dreamer do you represent?

- Can you suggest any new actions for the dreamer to take in their waking lives?

- What do you have to tell the dreamer about new ways to grow and love?

- Is there something else that you wish to share with the dreamer at this time, or do you feel as though this conversation is complete?

When this conversation is complete, begin to release this character's energy from your total focus. As you do so, recognize that this character represents one part of yourself . . . you can continue to explore this part of you, nurture it, and transform it once your focus returns to your waking life . . . For now, just embrace this character as one aspect of your being and return to a deeper awareness of your whole body and spirit . . . Then when you are ready, gently open your eyes.

Dreamer and Listener

Take a little time to share. Then switch roles and begin this adventure again.

Picking up the Thread for Friends

This adventure can help you to identify the unifying threads or themes that tie a dream together.

Preparation

Each of you may need to skim over Themes on page 55 so you both have a basic understanding of parallels, contrasts, and themes before you begin this adventure.

Adventure

One person shares a dream out loud. The other one listens. Both of you look for parallels, contrasts, and strong images within the dream. Then you can discuss the themes that you see — the patterns and relationships within the dream. See if you can both come up with several titles for the dream. Share these. Then switch roles so that whomever has not shared a dream yet, can do so.

Free Association for Partners

In this waking dream adventure, the two of you create a variety of images based on one theme.

Preparation

Select a theme you would like to explore together. You can pick a theme from your dreams or choose one of the themes listed.

Suggested Themes

Growth	Peace	Art
Health	Flight	Wisdom
Trust	Completion	Humor
Change	Beginnings	Love
Beauty	Endings	Imagination

Adventure

Read over the whole text before you start this adventure. To begin, each of you closes your eyes and focuses on the theme.

Pay attention to the images, feelings, messages, sounds, and sensations that you experience as you focus on this theme. Share these out loud. Take several minutes with this. Next, each of you does your own silent, personal version of this dream, such as "I am at peace," or "my health." Once again, take several minutes to do this.

Then take turns describing the personal version of your theme, using one of the images listed below.

a garden	a fairy tale	an old woman
a theater	a meal	a castle
a path	a little boy	a new technology
a light source	a farm	animals
a painting	a class	a community
a cup	a mountain place	

For example, if your theme was "my wisdom," one of you would repeat the words "my wisdom" to yourself and imagine a garden that reflects this phrase. Then you would describe the garden out loud to your partner. (The garden you described would be a symbol of your own wisdom.) When you were done, your partner would contemplate the words "my wisdom" and imagine a theater that he or she feels represents those words. Then your partner would describe this theater to you.

Continue taking turns using different images from the list, until you both feel that you have explored this theme thoroughly. Then breathe deeply and release this image from your focus. Open your eyes when you feel ready.

This adventure demonstrates the process through which dreams are formed. When you sleep, your inner being chooses a theme about which you need to learn, and then creates a variety of images — like gardens, theaters, and castles — that help to teach you about this theme.

The more you practice this adventure, the more you will come to understand the process of dreaming itself. At the same time, you will also be giving yourselves the fun of dreaming together!

10
My Own Dream Journey

Several years ago, I was interviewed by a woman named Marion from a local radio station. I decided to include that interview here so that I could share my own process of discovering and exploring dreams with you. I hope that, in some way, it provides you with a little inspiration as you seek to bring your own dreams to life.

Interview

Marion: When and how did you first get involved with dream journeys?

Ana Lora: I first discovered dreams in a woman's journal writing class. The teacher offered extra credit if we explored a dream and then shared our exploration with the class. That's how I got started with all of this. After exploring just one dream, I found I couldn't stop. I wanted to examine others and I wanted to know more about dreams in general. So I began reading all the dream books I could get my hands on and delving into more of my own dreams. Then gradually I started helping friends examine theirs, too.

In those days, I explored dreams the way we had explored fish in my college biology class. In that class, a group of us would each be given a dead fish. We'd dissect the carcass on a laboratory table, identify all the organs, and then grin at each other across all the slimy parts, confident that we knew all about fish.

I explored dreams in exactly that same way. I would take a dream apart, and label all the little pieces, but still I didn't understand that dream as a whole and I had no sense of what dreams themselves were really all about. The little pieces of dreams sparkled and glimmered like little gems, but I had no idea how to take them into my heart or my life. Yet around that time, I decided to teach.

Marion: What was your teaching experience like?

Ana Lora: Well, as I said, I started teaching with a little knowledge about dreams, and virtually no experience or understanding. I did, however, have a great deal of intensity, curiosity, and excitement about the subject, and this helped to carry me along.

At first, I helped others to explore their dreams the way I explored mine, the "dead fish approach." I pointed out parallels in their dreams, and then helped individuals to examine those parallels, so that they could label what was going on within their dreams. Yet I still felt that something was missing in what I was doing.

Only gradually did I begin to realize what the missing link was. I needed to emphasize *feeling* dream images more and *thinking* about them less. I needed to trust my intuition more in the process of understanding dreams. As I learned to trust my own feelings more, I found that I could absorb the meaning of each dream more fully. My understanding seemed more whole, less fragmented. I also began to see that dream images had very real messages in them that could help us in our lives. And all of this became a part of my teaching.

Marion: What happened with your teaching after that?

Ana Lora: Then I moved to California and my classes took on a whole different flavor. They got quite a bit livelier — even wild and crazy, at times. I was becoming more and more excited about dreams and dream journeys all the time, and I think I infected many of my students with that same excitement (even though none of us were really sure what we were excited about). Imagine a big group of delighted-looking people moving down the road at a fast trot, having no clear idea where they're going, and you'll be able to picture my dream classes. We talked about our own dreams, drew cartoons of each other's dreams, made up poems, stories, and puppet shows, and put on masks and costumes and acted our dreams out.

Then my father died. That devastated me so much that I did not teach for awhile. When I did start teaching again, I slowed the pace of my classes down quite a bit. We embarked on fewer adventures with our dreams, but each adventure we entered into, we entered into more deeply. And it became safe to cry as well as laugh in my classes. This came about because I stopped being afraid of discovering feelings of sadness or hurt in myself or in others. I still welcomed the sense of delight and playfulness that ran rampant in my early classes, but I encouraged my students to explore the disappointment and unhappiness indicated by certain dream images, too.

You see, when I went through the process of accepting my father's death, I learned that I had to move through my sadness and my pain in order to find my joy and delight. I realized that our spirits are not free until our hearts are. And although I had already begun to consider the dream journey a spiritual one, at this time I also realized that it is very much a journey into our hearts, our humanness, and our deepest feelings. I began to see my role as a dream teacher more and more as one of a gentle guide, assisting others on the journey into their hearts. So exploring all kinds of feelings associated with dream images became the central part of my teaching.

Marion: Mmm . . . Now, let's talk more about your personal dream experiences. What are some of the ways you've incorporated dreams into your own life?

Ana Lora: Mostly they've given me glimpses of magic and then I've tried to follow up on that magic. For instance, when I first planned to move to California, I had a dream that I was going to meet a special man named Robert. So I intended to keep my eyes peeled for a "Robert" when I came here.

One of the first things I did when I got here was to take a workshop with Peter Caddy, one of the founders of the Findhorn Community in Northern Scotland. When I arrived at that workshop, a man with gentle eyes, gray hair, and a red beard, came over and talked to me. "This must be Robert," I thought. I introduced myself to the man and asked his name. "My name is Foster," he said. I felt confused. I'd been sure that was he!

During the lunchtime break in the workshop, Foster, two others from the workshop, and I decided to go to a restaurant in town. We had a nice lunch. I sat next to a man named Kevin and talked to him about the workshop. Midway through our conversation however, I stopped listening and stared across the table in amazement. Foster was telling the woman sitting next to him, "Well, Foster isn't really my first name, you see. It's actually my last name, but I use it as my first name. My first name is really Robert."

In the weeks following that workshop, Robert and I got to know each other, and now he's one of my dearest friends. As it turned out, he had had a dream that he was going to meet a special, dark-haired woman and he saw himself walking over a bridge with her . . .

By following up on suggestions offered in my dreams, like that one with Foster, I've allowed my dreams to create some magic in my life. I've started conversations with people I've dreamed about or tried out some activity in which I saw myself participating in a dream . . . and then, little by little, my dreams have begun to change my life in a gentle, good way. I've relied on my dreams to help me take little steps towards a deeper sense of peace and happiness. And I try to encourage my students to allow their dreams to work this kind of magic in their lives, too.

Marion: Do you still participate in dream adventures, like the ones in this book?

Ana Lora: Yes, I try to embark upon some dream adventures at least several times a week. It is my form of meditation, really. I feel that I speak to the most ancient part of my being through my dreams, and that this part of me can guide me in my life. The more attention I pay to this guidance, the more happy I become.

Marion: What do you say to someone who says to you, "Be practical . . . dreams aren't practical"?

Ana Lora: I tell them that sometimes I've learned new things and discovered new work opportunities by following tips from my dreams.

For instance, at one time in my waking life, I was looking for someone to do calligraphy on the posters I was using to advertise my dream classes. I kept calling one woman on the phone, but I couldn't get a hold of her. Then, one night, I dreamed that I could do my own calligraphy. I even dreamed about the type of pen I should use. It was not a pen I'd ever seen before, in waking life. But when I woke up, I thought to myself, "What have I got to lose? I'm

going to go to an art store and see if they have any of those pens."
So I did. And the store did have pens like the one I dreamed about.
The package they came in even had a booklet with instructions on
how to do basic calligraphy! Eager to try them out, I bought them
and hurried home.

My first attempts were passable. The letters were a little
wobbly, a little squarish, and a little stiff. Yet, in time my calligraphy improved and in the years that followed several institutions
and private individuals actually employed me to do some lettering
for them.

In another such instance, I dreamed about seniors and
handicapped folks for three nights in a row. A voice in one of the
dreams told me that I would be rewarded if I would let some of
these people get into the back seat of my car. When I woke up, I
realized that this was a suggestion for me to get a part-time job
working with older folks. I had worked as an activity director a few
years before when I was living in Portland, and had approached the
senior center in my area when I first moved to California, but they
didn't have any work for me at that time. After having this dream,
however, I decided to try calling them again.

"Ana Garrard?!!!!" the voice said incredulously, on the
other end of the phone. "The activity director here just announced
that she wanted to cut back her hours, so as of today, we are looking for another part-time activity director. We were just trying to
find your resume, so we could call you!" They were as amazed as I
was by the pattern of events. Before the phone conversation was
over, I had a new job.

Usually what we mean when we evaluate the "practicality"
of something is "can we make money at it?" My answer to this
question, in regard to dreams, is *yes*. For too long we have sepa-
rated the spirit world from the physical world. Our dreams can def-
initely speak to us about money issues (and about the underlying
issues that affect the flow of money in our lives). There is no way
for us to achieve greater wealth than through embracing our own
spirits.

Marion: What role do you think dreams play in our culture today?

Ana Lora: A healing one . . . our society is greatly in need of healing. We, as a culture, have fostered institutions and lifestyles that exclude the dream state, that don't encourage us to discover our own truths, or to explore the love and light within ourselves. That is why there is so much drug use, so many stress diseases, and the feeling of emptiness among people today. We know we are missing something, but we don't know how to reconnect with our own vibrancy, or our own spirits. So now we need to find some tools to help us do that. A dream journey is one of those tools.

Marion: What relationship do you think dreams have to other healing methods?

Ana Lora: Well, its interesting that you should ask that. There was a time in my life, a few years ago, when I took a deeper look at the relationship between dreams and other healing methods. At that time, I didn't feel that I wanted to teach specifically about "dreams" any more.

I realized that what I was really interested in exploring were the questions, "How do we find our own creativity, delve into it, and learn to express it in physical form?" and "How can we face the challenges of living in a fluid, open way?" I realized that this was the core, the essence of my work. And that I wanted to be able to explore these questions with people who didn't remember their dreams, as well as those who did.

So I began teaching "healing" workshops and engaging in individual "healing" sessions with people. In the workshops I taught that healing involved choosing some focus that would help you to release energy — whether that focus was your breath, energy points in your body, physical movements or sounds, visualizations, your dreams, or whatever. Once energy was released, the healing process was begun (and would continue, naturally, by itself, given a supportive, nurturing atmosphere).

We discussed this idea in my workshops and then we practiced simple healing techniques based on the breath and some loosely guided imagery. I found that the kinds of experiences people had when participating in these activities were very similar to the experiences my students had when engaging in many of the dream adventures I teach.

Marion: So did you continue teaching "healing workshops" for awhile?

Ana Lora: I did a few workshops, but most of my work during this time was focused on some very intense sessions with individuals. And these sessions were very interesting, because I'd just jumped into "healing work" the same way I'd jumped into dream journeys years before. I didn't really know what I was getting into.

Most often when people came to me to learn about dream journeys, they came because they wanted to discover new dimensions of themselves. When people came to me for healing, however, they usually came because they had experienced some kind of trauma in their waking lives that they needed to move through. I tried to assist them in this process, through breath work, visualization, some simple massage, guided dream adventures, and whatever else seemed like it might work at the moment! But I wasn't always prepared for the results.

I remember the first time I ever worked with someone who had a lot of rage, sadness, and frustrated love to release, who'd been abused as a child. We were exploring a dream symbol for the feelings she'd had at that time, when — whomp! — all this pent-up energy exploded out of her and hit me right in the face. I almost fell over backwards. My hands and cheeks got all tingly. I felt like I'd been hit by a strong blast of wind. "So this is healing," I thought. "Powerful stuff!"

Through time, I became a little more prepared for some of the results of this kind of work (although I found that everyone responded to it differently). I worked with people who had physical ailments, depression, a history of child abuse, symptoms of unwanted pregnancy, and cancer. As I encouraged people to relax and open up enough to regain access to their inner resources, the results were incredible.

The effect this kind of work had on me was incredible, too. When I was working with someone, I felt as though we became two parts of the same being — I was the part in front, shining the light on the path ahead of us, while they were the part that gathered the courage to meet what lay ahead. I was endlessly and profoundly moved by the kind of courage I witnessed in other human beings.

But a time came for me when I could no longer be just the beacon for other spirits. As I continued to practice healing work through time, I began to feel an increasing pressure building up within myself. I finally realized what this pressure was when I had a dream in which a voice said to me, "If you wish to do more healing work, you must integrate healing more fully into your own life."

That stopped me cold. I realized that this statement was very true and that I had been avoiding it. I needed to make some very real changes in my life in order to move on with my own healing process. During the months that followed, I totally restructured my life. I moved to a new house, ended a relationship with a man, quit my part-time job, and began to create paintings once again.

Then one day when I was out painting landscapes and kept botching canvas after canvas, I began to feel this strange sensation, as if someone were tugging at the corner of my painting smock. I ignored it for a time, but finally I turned and asked that invisible presence, "What do you want??!!" "Writing," it said. "You are supposed to be writing." Surprised, I laid down my paintbrush, returned to my house, and pulled out a paper and pen. Whoosh! Immediately this book began to come out on paper.

Marion: So your book took off at that point?

Ana Lora: Yes, it did. I think I'd had a major portion of this book in my head for a few years, but I had never tried to put it down on paper. Once I did, that was a turning point in my life.

During the months that followed, I would often go to the same restaurant to have breakfast, early in the morning. I'd order french toast and coffee, and sit and write my book on dreams while other people's conversations came floating in and out of my awareness. Those early days of writing were especially exciting. I think I was always breathless and my eyes were always sparkling. (And this was not just because of the french toast and the six cups of coffee.) I think I was so vibrant, because finally I was really letting my own spirit speak. I was recording what it was that I saw and thought and felt, the bits of "knowing" that had been buried deep inside me for years. It was as though I'd been growing some big, bushy plants in a dark, quiet closet and now was finally bringing them out into the light, so they could flower.

Every day I went forward and set my own words down on paper. Sometimes I'd imagine that there was a big group of people listening to what I wrote, and that made me feel good, because then I didn't feel like I was doing this project alone. And sometimes as I wrote, I'd just be aware that I myself was listening to what I had to say, and that was enough.

In one of the Carlos Castaneda books, the teacher named Don Juan says that you can cultivate inner strength by committing yourself to one activity that you will carry out every day. I saw the truth of this statement as I worked on my book, because I noticed myself feeling stronger, happier, and more confident every day.

Marion: So this book sounds like "the realization of a dream" for you. Did you find realizing this dream to be an easy process?

Ana Lora: Not at all. Lots of times I struggled with it. When I first tried to refine my writing on the typewriter, I almost went crazy looking at the little black words on the white paper. Just looking at the typewritten words would cause me to forget that it was *my* book that I was writing and that I could write it any way I chose. I'd start thinking about describing my dream ideas to a bunch of Harvard professors and I'd assume an authoritative, intellectual stance in a matter of seconds. Then I'd worry about whether my book would be successful or not. Pretty soon my neck would start hurting, and then my eyes, and I'd start squirming in front of the typewriter. I only got relief from the struggle of writing gradually, as I learned to give myself more freedom in what I was doing.

Sometimes giving myself more freedom meant giving myself good, long breaks from the writing. I needed to paint, draw, talk to people, take walks, and breathe in the life that I was writing about. Otherwise I'd get so focused on working on my book and trying to get all the words just right that I'd start feeling dizzy and cut off from the life source that fed me.

At other times, giving myself more freedom meant changing the way I looked at the book itself. I had to be willing to use my book as a tool for discovering who I was — what I had to say and how I wanted to say it. I had to learn to shed expectations, styles, and thoughts that I'd adopted from other people along the way. This took time and patience on my part. Finally, however, I did begin to see real, strong glimmers of my own spirit in my work. Then I knew the biggest part of the struggle was over. My dream was coming true.

Marion: Do you have any advice for a person who is trying to "realize a dream" in their own lives?

Ana Lora: Well, realizing a dream usually puts you face to face with yourself. You are going to have to learn to face yourself, and accept yourself, before your dreams can come true. We must not value our creations more than ourselves. If we do persist in this, manifesting dreams can become a struggle.

Each of us has a spirit within us, a truth, a vision of beauty and wisdom that we are here to express. And each of us also has humanness inside us, a need to bring that vision into focus one step at a time, with love. We must honor both of these parts of ourselves, and not be afraid of them. They can both work together. We must remember as we seek to create, however, that the creation in the physical world takes time, that it has limitations, that we must be trusting and patient with ourselves.

I've had this big hang-up with perfection, myself, that has often caused me to trip over my own feet. I've been afraid of starting projects because I've been afraid of making "mistakes" . . . and then once I've started them, I've been afraid of calling them finished, because I can see they're not perfect.

Luckily, I'm finally getting over this! One person who helped me to get over this was the author Ursula LeGuin. I was looking at one of her early books once, when I realized two things, with amazement. One was that the book was very clearly flawed. The other was that it also had great beauty within it. As I stood there, book in hand, I realized just how grateful I was to Ms. LeGuin that she had gone ahead and published that book — flaws and beauty and all. Because if she hadn't been brave enough to do that, if she had waited for the book to be "completely perfect" before publishing it — then I would probably not have had it, or many of her other wonderful books to read. She might still be working on creating her one and only masterpiece and the world of books would be a lot less colorful than it is right now.

Marion: How do you think working to "realize your dreams" relates to "seeking to understand your nighttime dreams"?

Ana Lora: Oh, they're intricately connected. When people seek to understand their nighttime dreams, they begin to gain insight into themselves. They start to learn what truly has meaning for them.

When people talk about manifesting a dream, they're usually talking about taking action in the physical world to try and create something that has meaning for them. This could be an action like making a work of art, forming a new relationship with someone, taking a trip up into the mountains, or some other event like that.

One of these ways of exploring dreams seems to have more of an emphasis on "healing," while the other has more of an emphasis on "creating." Yet this is the old story of the yin and the yang, the male and the female. Really, they're one and the same. One leads to the other. Once you gain new insights into yourself, how can you help but create, based on these new insights? Once you engage in a journey that helps you to remember the deepest dreams and desires within you, how can you help but seek to bring those dreams into physical form?

I don't think you can have true healing without creation accompanying it. We must replace old visions, old ways of doing things, with new ones. Deeper insight naturally flows into deeper, heartfelt action. We are both spirit and substance, after all. Once the healing dream journeys that we participate in get us in touch with what we love, our creations are the natural expression of that love, the way we honor it.

Marion: How do you see your own dream journey now? And do you see dreams playing a strong role in your life in the future?

Ana Lora: To me, a dream is no longer a separate "thing" or "idea." The willingness, buried within each of us, to follow our imagination, to breathe freely, to open our hearts, and to meet the eternal in any form — that is the dream to me. It is the line I want to trace with my fingers, the thread that holds my life together at the seams and gives it meaning.

I suppose I could teach anything now — a yoga class, a painting class, a dance class — and it would still be a dream class to me. Yet, I still do like to use nighttime dreams specifically as tools in my teaching. These kinds of dreams give us wonderful entryways into many kinds of new creations — new writings, new songs, new paintings, new recipes, new friendships, new dances — all of that. Also, when you are trying to understand your dreams, you are immediately faced with the challenge of seeing yourself as a whole being. You learn that you are a sparkling spirit, a body with sensations, a person with thoughts and feelings, a part of trees, cats, turtles, and the rest of the universe. Exploring dreams helps you to see this, to establish all the bits and pieces of your own wisdom.

I can think of few tasks I enjoy more than helping others to recognize their own wisdom. As each of us learns to recognize our own wisdom, I think we become capable of touching one another more deeply, of responding with love. In this way, we set ourselves on the road to all those good things we always talk about — like joy, trust, creativity, happiness, and peace. Since I want my life and others' to be filled with these kinds of good things, I suppose I will be exploring dreams and teaching others to explore them for a long time to come.

STAY IN TOUCH

On the following pages you will find listed, with their current prices, some of the books now available on related subjects. Your book dealer stocks most of these and will stock new titles in the Llewellyn series as they become available. We urge your patronage.

To obtain our full catalog, to keep informed about new titles as they are released and to benefit from informative articles and helpful news, you are invited to write for our bi-monthly news magazine/catalog, *Llewellyn's New Worlds of Mind and Spirit*. A sample copy is free, and it will continue coming to you at no cost as long as you are an active mail customer. Or you may subscribe for just $10.00 in U.S.A. and Canada ($20.00 overseas, first class mail). Many bookstores also have *New Worlds* available to their customers. Ask for it.

Stay in touch! In *New Worlds'* pages you will find news and features about new books, tapes and services, announcements of meetings and seminars, articles helpful to our readers, news of authors, products and services, special money-making opportunities, and much more.

Llewellyn's New Worlds of Mind and Spirit
P.O. Box 64383-253, St. Paul, MN 55164-0383, U.S.A.

*　*　*

TO ORDER BOOKS AND TAPES

If your book dealer does not have the books described on the following pages readily available, you may order them direct from the publisher by sending full price in U.S. funds, plus $3.00 for postage and handling for orders *under* $10.00; $4.00 for orders *over* $10.00. There are no postage and handling charges for orders over $50.00. Postage and handling rates are subject to change. UPS Delivery: We ship UPS whenever possible. Delivery guaranteed. Provide your street address as UPS does not deliver to P.O. Boxes. UPS to Canada requires a $50.00 minimum order. Allow 4-6 weeks for delivery. Orders outside the U.S.A. and Canada: Airmail—add retail price of book; add $5.00 for each non-book item (tapes, etc.); add $1.00 per item for surface mail.

FOR GROUP STUDY AND PURCHASE

Because there is a great deal of interest in group discussion and study of the subject matter of this book, we feel that we should encourage the adoption and use of this particular book by such groups by offering a special quantity price to group leaders or agents.

Our Special Quantity Price for a minimum order of five copies of *An Invitation to Dream* is $38.85 cash-with-order. This price includes postage and handling within the United States. Minnesota residents must add 6.5% sales tax. For additional quantities, please order in multiples of five. For Canadian and foreign orders, add postage and handling charges as above. Credit card (VISA, MasterCard, American Express) orders are accepted. Charge card orders only ($15.00 minimum order) may be phoned in free within the U.S.A. or Canada by dialing 1-800-THE-MOON. For customer service, call 1-612-291-1970. Mail orders to:

LLEWELLYN PUBLICATIONS
P.O. Box 64383-253, St. Paul, MN 55164-0383, U.S.A.

DREAM ALCHEMY
Shaping Our Dreams to Transform Our Lives
by Ted Andrews

What humanity is rediscovering is that what we dream can become real. Learning to shift the dream to reality and the reality to dream—to walk the thread of life between the worlds—to become a shapeshifter, a dreamwalker, is available to all. We have the potential to stimulate dream awareness for greater insight and fulfillment, higher inspiration and ultimately even controlled out-of-body experiences. It is all part of the alchemical process of the soul.

Through the use of our ancient myths and tales, we can initiate a process of dream alchemy. Through control of the dream state and its energies, we are put in touch with realities and energies that can open us to greater productivity during our waking hours. Learn to alter sleep conditions and increase dream activity through the use of herbs, fragrances, crystals, flower essences, totems, talismans and mandalas.

For those just opening to the psychic and spiritual realms, this is one of the safest and easiest ways to bridge your consciousness to higher realms.

0-897542-017-6, 264 pgs., 6 x 9, illus., softcover $12.95

THE DREAM LOVER
Transforming Relationships Through Dreams
by Les Peto

Every man has an inner female. Every woman has an inner male. Your "other half," or "Dream Lover," visits you in your dreams nightly. She, or he, presents the mysteries of your waking-hour relationships: their complexities, confusions and fascinations. Most importantly, when you work on your relationships through your Dream Lover, you are working on yourself and your own hidden truths.

Learn to summon your Dream Lover with new and effective psychological techniques. Commune with your Dream Lover every night. Discover where Dream Lovers comes from, what it means when you encounter them in a nightmare, and how you can make them your ally. Get answers to confusing relationship and sexuality issues. Use these dreams for personal growth and change, no matter what your age or stage in life

The opposite sex offers an enduring symbol of the unknown, a constant challenge to learn more and go further into the unrealized unconscious self. Your Dream Lover will lead you to wherever you need to go.

87542-595-X, 192 pgs., 6 x 9, softcover $9.95

All prices subject to change without notice.

DREAMS & WHAT THEY MEAN TO YOU
by Migene Gonzalez Wippler

Everyone dreams. Yet dreams are rarely taken seriously—they seem to be only a bizarre series of amusing or disturbing images that the mind creates for no particular purpose. Yet dreams, through a language of their own, contain essential information about ourselves which, if properly analyzed and understood, can change our lives. In this fascinating and well-written book, the author gives you all of the information needed to begin interpreting—even creating—your own dreams.

Dreams & What They Mean To You begins by exploring the nature of the human mind and consciousness, then discusses the results of the most recent scientific research on sleep and dreams. The author analyzes different types of dreams: telepathic, nightmares, sexual and prophetic. In addition, there is an extensive Dream Dictionary which lists the meanings for a wide variety of dream images.

Most importantly, Gonzalez-Wippler tells you how to practice creative dreaming—consciously controlling dreams as you sleep. Once a person learns to control his dreams, his horizons will expand and his chances of success will increase!

0-87542-288-8, 240 pgs., mass market   **$3.95**

MAGICKAL DANCE
Your Body as an Instrument of Power
by Ted Andrews

Choreograph your own evolution through one of the most powerful forms of magickal ritual: Dance. When you let your inner spirit express itself through movement, you can fire your vitality, revive depleted energies, awaken individual creativity and transcend your usual perceptions.

Directed physical movement creates electrical changes in the body that create shifts in consciousness. It links the hemispheres of the brain, joining the rational and the intuitive to create balance, healing, strength and psychic energy.

This book describes and illustrates over 20 dance and other magickal movements and postures. Learn to shapeshift through dance, dance your prayers into manifestation, align with the planets through movement, activate and raise the kundalini, create group harmony and power, and much more. Anyone who can move any part of the body can perform magical movement. No formal dance training is required.

0-87542-004-4, 224 pgs., 6 x 9, illus., photos, softcover $9.95

All prices subject to change without notice.

THE PSYCHIC SIDE OF DREAMS
by Hans Holzer

Wakefulness and the dream state go hand in hand, equal partners in our day-to-day existence, sharing consciousness, and forming and two halves of our lives. *The Psychic Side of Dreams* (newly reprinted with added material) acquaints readers with the true nature of the dream state, the many aspects of dreaming, and how to open the dream channel so wide that it serves as a secondary (or superior) world of perception.

Illustrated with numerous case histories from people around the world, *The Psychic Side of Dreams* explains the different types of dreams: anxiety dreams, out-of-body experiences ("falling dreams"), nightmares, prophetic dreams (in which future events are foreseen or foretold), warning dreams (in which future events are depicted so that we can alter the results), survival dreams (including communication with the world beyond or with the dead), ESP dreams (psychic dreams that relate to events taking place at exactly the same moment), reincarnation dreams and recurrent dreams.

Everyone dreams, everyone can learn to interpret dreams, and we can all use dreams to expand knowledge and control of our lives. Hans Holzer's objective and documented investigation will show you how you can, too.

0-87542-369-8, 288 pgs., mass market   **$4.95**

SECRETS OF GYPSY DREAM READING
by Raymond Buckland, Ph.D.

The Gypsies have carried their arcane wisdom and time-tested methods of dream interpretation around the world. Now, in *Secrets of Gypsy Dream Reading*, Raymond Buckland, a descendant of the Romani Gypsies, reveals these fascinating methods.

Learn how to accurately interpret dreams, dream the future, dream for profit, remember your dreams more clearly, and willfully direct your dreams. The Gypsies' observations on dreaming are extremely perceptive and enlightening. They say that dreams are messages, giving advice on what is most beneficial for you. Many times these messages could mean the difference between happiness and misery—if not life and death.

In today's fast-paced, often superficial world, we need to listen to the Gypsies' words of wisdom more than ever. Listen to your dreams and achieve success, riches, better health—and more—in your waking hours!

0-87542-086-9, 224 pgs., mass market, illus.   **$3.95**

All prices subject to change without notice.

THE LLEWELLYN PRACTICAL GUIDE TO CREATIVE VISUALIZATION
by Denning & Phillips

All things you will ever want must have their start in your mind. The average person uses very little of the full creative power that is his, potentially. It's like the power locked in the atom—it's all there, but you have to learn to release it and apply it constructively.

IF YOU CAN SEE IT ... in your Mind's Eye ... you will have it! It's true: you can have whatever you want, but there are "laws" to mental creation that must be followed. The power of the mind is not limited to, nor limited by, the material world. *Creative Visualization* enables Man to reach beyond, into the invisible world of Astral and Spiritual Forces.

Some people apply this innate power without actually knowing what they are doing, and achieve great success and happiness; most people, however, use this same power, again unknowingly, incorrectly, and experience bad luck, failure, or at best an unfulfilled life.

This book changes that. Through an easy series of step-by-step, progressive exercises, your mind is applied to bring desire into realization! Wealth, power, success, happiness even psychic powers ... even what we call magickal power and spiritual attainment ..: all can be yours. You can easily develop this completely natural power, and correctly apply it, for your immediate and practical benefit. Illustrated with unique, "puts-you-into-the-picture" visualization aids.

0-87542-183-0, 294 pgs., 5 1/4 x 8, illus., softcover $8.95

THE COMPLETE HANDBOOK OF NATURAL HEALING
by Marcia Starck

Got an itch that won't go away? Want a massage but don't know the difference between Rolfing, Reichian Therapy and Reflexology? Tired of going to the family doctor for minor illnesses that you know you could treat at home—if you just knew how?

Designed to function as a home reference guide (yet enjoyable and interesting enough to be read straight through), this book addresses all natural healing modalities in use today: dietary regimes, nutritional supplements, cleansing and detoxification, vitamins and minerals, herbology, homeopathic medicine and cell salts, traditional Chinese medicine, Ayurvedic medicine, body work therapies, exercise, mental and spiritual therapies, and more. In addition, a section of 41 specific ailments outlines natural treatments for everything from acne to varicose veins.

0-87542-742-1, 416 pgs., 6 x 9, softcover $12.95

All prices subject to change without notice.

THE SECRET OF LETTING GO
by Guy Finley

Whether you need to let go of a painful heartache, a destructive habit, a frightening worry or a nagging discontent, *The Secret of Letting Go* shows you how to call upon your own hidden powers and how they can take you through and beyond any challenge or problem. This book reveals the secret source of a brand-new kind of inner strength.

In the light of your new and higher self-understanding, emotional difficulties such as loneliness, fear, anxiety and frustration fade into nothingness as you happily discover they never really existed in the first place.

With a foreword by Desi Arnaz Jr., and introduction by Dr. Jesse Freeland, *The Secret of Letting Go* is a pleasing balance of questions and answers, illustrative examples, truth tales, and stimulating dialogues that allow the reader to share in the exciting discoveries that lead up to lasting self-liberation.

This is a book for the discriminating, intelligent, and sensitive reader who is looking for *real* answers.

0-87542-223-3, 240 pgs., 5 1/4 x 8, softcover $9.95

MOVING WITH THE WIND
Magick and Healing in the Martial Arts
Brian Crowley with Esther Crowley

Tap into the incredible and mysterious force that can empower you to attain perfect mental control and spiritual enlightenment, perform bodily healing through invisible means, live a prolonged and vigorous life ... or even cut a pile of bricks in half with a bare fist. This mysterious power is the fundamental secret that lies at the foundation of all esoteric systems. It is the control of pranic energies, of the force known simply as "chi," which is said to permeate and motivate all things throughout the universe.

Against a backdrop that traces the spiritual philosophy, history and development of major martial art forms, *Moving with the Wind* explores the origin and nature of this intrinsic but still occult and magickal (to Western science at least) chi force that underlies all the oriental fighting forms—and offers a set of easy-to-follow exercises—with special emphasis on the healing arts sometimes associated with martial arts activity—that will help you develop your own chi reservoir for practical daily use, or to prepare yourself for martial arts training.

0-87542-134-2, 192 pgs., 5 1/4 x 8, illus., softcover $10.00

All prices subject to change without notice.

WHAT YOUR DREAMS CAN TEACH YOU
by Alex Lukeman
Dreams are honest and do not lie. They have much to teach us, but
the lessons are often difficult to understand. Confusion comes not
from the dream but from the outer mind's attempt to understand it.

What Your Dreams Can Teach You is a workbook of self-discovery, with
a systematic and proven approach to the understanding of dreams. It
does not contain lists of meanings for dream symbols. Only you, the
dreamer, can discover what the images in your dreams mean for you.
The book *does* contain step-by-step information which can lead you
to success with your dreams, success that will bear fruit in your waking hours. Learn to tap into the aspect of yourself that truly knows
how to interpret dreams, the inner energy of understanding called
the "Dreamer Within." This aspect of your consciousness will lead
you to an accurate understanding of your dreams and even assist you
with interpreting dreams of others.
0-87542-475-9, 288 pgs., 6 x 9, softcover   **$12.95**

PERSONAL ALCHEMY
A Handbook of Healing & Self-Transformation
by Amber Wolfe
Personal Alchemy offers the first bold look at the practical use of "Rays"
for healing and self-development. Rays are spontaneous energy ema-
nations emitting a specific quality, property or attribute. The Red Ray,
for example, represents the energies of life force, survival and
strength. When used in conjunction with active imagery, the alchemical properties of the Red Ray can activate independence, release infe-
riority, or realign destructiveness and frustration. *Personal Alchemy*
explains each color Ray and Light in depth, in a manner designed to
teach the material and to encourage the active participation of the
reader.

What's more, this book goes beyond anything else written on the
Rays because it contains an extensive set of alchemical correlations
that amplify the Ray's powers. Each Ray correlates with a specific
element, harmonic sound, aroma, symbol, person, rune, astrological
sign, Tarot card, angel, and stone, so there are numerous ways to
experience and learn this system of healing magick.
0-87542-890-8, 592 pgs., 7 x 10, illus., softcover   **$17.95**

All prices subject to change without notice.

APPLIED VISUALIZATION
A Mind-Body Program
by James Lynn Page

Unleash your creative force! Here is a practical program that you can use to achieve your dreams, whether material, emotional or spiritual. *Applied Visualization* is the first *in-depth* study of a practice that is widely used by therapists and laypersons alike. It is described under various terminology: active imagination, creative visualization and guided imagery.

In easily accessible language, this book explains how the laws of nature forge mind/matter relationships. By working with the symbols and images of the unconscious and the inner worlds, you will discover how your desires do in fact bring on outer events. In other words, if you can think it, you can have it!

Intrigued by the creative process? *Applied Visualization* presents a full report of an enquiry into the nature of the mind. Discover just how creative visualization works. Obtain the objects of personal desire. Unblock creative potential. Learn how to use visualization during a personal crisis. Follow the easy, Ten-step Visualization Workout.

0-87542-597-6, 144 pgs., 6 x 9, softcover   **$9.95**

BRIDGES TO SUCCESS & FULFILLMENT
Techniques to Discover & Release Your Potential
by William W. Hewitt

In the tradition of Dale Carnegie and Norman Vincent Peale, William Hewitt's latest book will make you stop and think seriously about yourself and your life. In his trademark easy-reading style, this former IBM executive and motivational trainer offers something *new* in the line of self-improvement: A blend of traditional and non-traditional techniques for dealing successfully with the changes, choices and stresses of our time.

Whether you are going through a divorce, loss of a job, a mid-life crisis, or simply want to get *more* out of life, *Bridges to Success & Fulfillment* provides the tools to build a happier tomorrow. Explore your life purpose, choices, altered states of consciousness, self hypnosis, meditation, prayer, self-talk, spirituality, astrology, dreams, difficult people, death, stretching your mind, committees, suicide, even good old boy networks. Hewitt's gutsy, humorous and common-sense approach will inspire you to take charge of your life, work with your higher consciousness, and begin to set in motion a future that is successful beyond your wildest dreams!

0-87542-323-X, 192 pgs., 5 1/4 x 8, illus., photos   **$7.95**

All prices subject to change without notice.